To Stan —
With thanks for your support
and friendship!

NINE LIVES ON FOUR COASTS

Autobiography/Confession/Love Story
Of an Educational Administrator)

Byron F. Evans

Prairie Publications
Urbana, Illinois
2004

TABLE OF CONTENTS

Foreword		1
Chapter One	First Scrapes in the Sucker State	5
Chapter Two	Look at Them Eyes	13
Chapter Three	Home of the Hot Dogs	19
Chapter Four	I Been Workin' on De Railroad	35
Chapter Five	Take Down Your Service Flag, Mother, Your Son's in the A S T P	47
Chapter Six	Lengthening the Oregon Trail	61
Chapter Seven	Big Frog, Little Pond	77
Chapter Eight	Back to School; Deliverance Again	95
Chapter Nine	The Town That Ford Built	113
Chapter Ten	Health, History and Horses	123
Chapter Eleven	RPI – Turbulent Years	133
Chapter Twelve	Back to the Superintendency	151
Chapter Thirteen	Retirement at Last	159
Chapter Fourteen	Some Thoughts on Boards; Make-Your-Own-Scholarship	171
Chapter Fifteen	Other Travel	175
Chapter Sixteen	No Longer Unmentionable	181
Chapter Seventeen	Our Growing Family Tree	189

ISBN 0-9625736-5-5

Foreword

After some eighty years of life, it appears to me that most "ordinary" people have been cheek to jowl with extraordinary events. If you can accept this assertion, you may forgive me for presuming to tell my own story.

Autobiography can be an exercise in egotism, not too different from autoeroticism. The former usually is distinguished by quantity. This admitted, I will try to maintain some objectivity by struggling to think in the third person. Early into the process, I have looked in the mirror and seen some grimaces. At times, my stance has approached holier-than-thou, and claimed principles have not always squared with performance.

However, I did try to avoid bedroom gossip, excepting my own - (Only joking-actually pretty tame) for various reasons: much gossip is incorrect; when correct, it is incomplete by not telling the entire background and motivation of participants; it is judgmental even though none of us could be certain of our own actions in like circumstances; and I promised brother Rupert that this would be a small book. I am much indebted to him for his patience and for sharing his expertise in writing and publishing (and many other fields).

On writing and reading the pages of my youthful indiscretion/ stupidity, I am grateful that our society makes allowances for youth when defining criminal behavior. Dumb kids sometimes do grow up and become responsible citizens.

My patient and loyal Peggy, sons Eric and Philip, their wives, Anne and Lisa, and grandchildren, Ryan, Katie, Andrew and Alison, as well as other family deserve much more space and credit than can be included in this small book, but if I have accomplished anything worthwhile, it is to have helped launch and shape this family.

Apologies to my distinguished brothers for any discrepancies in recollection, and for using space to report trivia rather than their many significant accomplishments, which certainly speak for themselves.

Philip was a captain in Naval Air Intelligence, gifted singer of folk ditties, duty officer the night of the Cuban missile crisis, finally serving with the strategic air command before we lost him much too soon to ALS (Gehrig's Disease).

Allen was an executive with Monsanto, a jewelry craftsman and a recipient of the Bronze Star for his beyond-the-lines service directing

RUPERT, ALLEN, BYRON, PHILIP - 1971

artillery fire. He was on the West Bank of the Rhine River while his 76th Field Artillery Battalion was softening German defenses in preparation for the historic crossing which helped convince the High Command to surrender. Taking up his position in a German inn, he received excellent service, perhaps because the natives were war-weary (and they may have respected his radio contact with a command post capable of delivering massive strikes).

Rupert was professor and Dean of the College of Education at the University of Illinois, author of textbooks on electronics and vocational education, member of presidential commissions on technological manpower, past president of educational organizations and a pioneer in distance learning. One semester in the early 1970s he weekly (or was it weakly?) took a University plane from Illinois, across Indiana to Lexington, Kentucky, where he lectured to students in a dozen towns in Appalachia via a satellite in South America.

The Travelers, Loren and Hazel, with Peggy

The title stems from my many close calls during our residence in six states located on the four maritime coasts of America – Great Lakes, Pacific, Atlantic and Gulf of Mexico – plus wartime assignments in California and Washington.

This does not pretend to be a pictorial record. Our thousands of photos are deteriorating at the same rate as the author, and many are transparencies which are not easily useable. The motley few included here simply illustrate a small sampling of the many incidents enumerated in the text. The twelve-point type is a concession to eyesight, mine and readers'.

For much of my life, I was the youngest this and the youngest that. Suddenly, I find myself among the true seniors, so this little book is dedicated to treasured relatives and friends who have gone ahead of us to that sweet sleep.

In addition to those mentioned elsewhere, sincere thanks to the many neighbors and other friends who have blessed our lives. They are innumerable, but include such names as Congleton, Kinsler, Cannon, Johnson, Cord, Pado, Pensmith, Palmer, Lowe, Penning, Gibson, Phillips, Ten Hagen, Farrell, Beeler, Graf, Mruz, Christiansen, Bush, Connell, Williamson, Cumming, Donohue, Palamountain, Nimsker, Gilday, Mathiesen, Costello, Harper, Aronstamm, Bickelhaupt, Eddy, Aldrich, Maxam, Powers, Tarrant, Bolster, Clements, Riley, Rowland, Moran, Burke, Nixon, Hollowood, Ryan, Westerdahl (who protected me from radical protesters) and Ramroth (who protected me from radical cops).

Special thanks to the marvelous executive secretaries who helped Peggy keep me out of trouble: Betty Jane Olsen, Angela Odmin, and Sandra Brady.

CHAPTER ONE – FIRST SCRAPES IN THE SUCKER STATE

My dear wife Peggy has announced more than once that I am cheap, and with minimal assistance from torture/interrogation, I admit to cheapness from day one. The 1926 receipt from St. Charles Hospital in Aurora, Illinois, proves that my total cost was $36.50, including a ten day vacation for my mother, Hazel Rupert Evans.

Every life is a series of accidents, but my crowning achievement may simply be the survival of early childhood. In addition to the usual childhood diseases, my music teacher mother and coal miner-electrician-garage owner-teacher father, Loran Nelson Evans (and older brothers Rupert and Allen) nursed or extricated me from at least the following: serious facial burns; collapse of a concrete cover into a partially filled cistern (mother somehow reached and retrieved me with one hand); trying to throw myself off a bluff along with a watermelon rind; a fall or push from a barn loft (landing with my spine across a steel water tank); being knocked down by a car; falling from a high-flying swing; the overturning of our canvas top Ford next to a spike-toothed harrow; a punctured foot, etc.

Along with survival, however, I was granted some early impressions that shaped my appreciation of family – beyond the obvious parental love, I learned that older brothers are more than tormentors. When I drove a tree root deeply between two toes, they somehow carried me a considerable distance to town and medical attention.

This perfect storm of accidents could relate to an absent-minded gene, my own exuberance (and my brothers') and a lifelong pattern of streaks of luck, good and bad. Perhaps the only lasting effect from this first streak was the burn which left its imprint on my cheek and probably on my personality. When I was about two years old, we experienced one of those crackling cold Illinois nights when the house creaked and the frost built up thick inside the windows and on the nail heads. The only source of heat for the summer cottage – temporary home was a coal stove, and we clustered about it. When my four-year-old brother climbed on the back of my high chair, it toppled over and trapped me against the hot stove. The burn healed, of course, but for the rest of my life I have been growing nearly accustomed to people innocently asking about my mark.

The scarring did have one by-product for my later work in human relations: it helped me experience in a small way the results of prejudice. When I was ready to enter service in World War II, I was amazed that I failed the Navy V-12 physical exam because of "facial disfiguration." At that time, the Navy was not only racially segregated, but also believed that anything less than a perfect face could prevent exercise of leadership. (My portfolio at age seventeen showed that I had been president of my class in high school, winner of an American Legion Award, delegate to Indiana Boys State, successful candidate for the fourth ranking office in the mock election at Boys State, and early selection for a men's honorary society at Purdue University.) The army was not so picky.

The rest of the carnage in this series took place in Marshall, Illinois, downstate from my birthplace at Aurora. The hotel sign at the junction of State Highway No. 1 and U.S. 40 (the old National Road) proclaimed this to be the "Crossroads of America," and we lived there!

In that same block of downtown real estate, across from a butcher who provided many a bone both for our dog and our soup kettle in those years of Great Depression, stood the Marshall Tire and Battery Shop. Dad had started it with superhuman second effort following the bankruptcy of a similar business in Terre Haute, Indiana. He never rested until he had paid every penny to every creditor, and without the help of his former partner. Marshall had plenty of customers, because batteries were so expensive that rebuilding was the preferred option. The problem was that they had no money to pay and Dad was not comfortable in browbeating.

When I heard my first off-color joke from the older kids, I ran down to the garage where Dad was under a car as usual. What a letdown it was when the story fell with a thud and lay there! I never tried again. Silence was Dad's most devastating weapon, but a stronger response was seen on a few occasions. When a pellet from a Christmas gift BB gun lodged in my cheek, Dad pounded the barrel of the gun beyond any possible further use.

My brothers, ages seven and ten, were charter members of the sensational "B Club" (for body) but I was told that my age of five would not admit me. This was my first encounter with discrimination, because they were glad to have little girls of my age. The opening meeting was under way when they permitted me to stay and watch rather than submit the discrimination case to Mother for mediation. Fortunately, the entire assembly was young enough that nothing went beyond the simplest stage of exploration. However, when some of the members reported home about the agenda, the club was quickly disbanded.

DOCTORS THREE

We turned once more to our boys-only battles with slingshots, inner tube guns and sugar cane spears. Dad found a little time to join us in such projects as a battery powered coaster wagon, but he struggled all day to hold his business, and studied every night until long after our bed time. From brother Rupert's memoirs, I was surprised to learn that Dad had been a tennis enthusiast (as I was), even building his own clay court before I was born. I do not recall ever seeing him play the game or watch me play. Most of his life was all work and no play until Mother finally nagged him into traveling with her, using money which she had earned and saved.

Taking the Bash to Phil

We knew that there were weekly conferences in which dollar bills were laid out on the kitchen table and allocated painfully, but we never went hungry or felt deprived. Only our neglected teeth gave any real evidence of the hard times.

In Marshall, I learned the thrill of performing in public in a brothers- three vocal act, including an appearance on the Tuscola radio station–quite a novelty at that time. Annually since 1978 we have dusted off our favorite, "Dr. Diet, Dr. Quiet, and Dr. Merryman" for our nationwide Bash or reunion of the descendants of Papu and Grandmother Rupert.

This tradition started when Blythe "Casey" Jones, husband of our Aunt Helen, was dying in Birmingham, Michigan. He convinced his family to postpone any service until the end of winter, and then to have a Bash. We have met in locations from coast to coast, usually with at least fifty in attendance. The high point always is the Saturday night talent show, with performers from infancy through second childhood, and themes ranging from juggling to bagpipes. The family includes considerable musical talent, so the experience is relatively painless even for those who choose not to perform.

About monthly, on Saturday afternoon, we would load up for the thirty-two mile trip to see our grandparents in the coal and clay region of Brazil, Indiana. The ritual included coasting across the state line, holding our noses when passing the gas works at Terre Haute, and stopping on the return trip to splurge two scarce dimes on hot salted peanuts and chocolate drops. Gasoline for the trip cost about thirty cents, and we always came back with a care package of food and other essentials from the grandparents.

Both sets of old folks (then in their late fifties, I suppose), lived in Bee Ridge, a rural area near Brazil. Our grandfathers were moderately successful self-made men who were living in semi-retirement, comfortably and with the general respect of their community.

Grandfather Rupert (Papu through the early mispronunciation by his first grandchild and my older brother Rupert) and our grandmother, Emma Downing Rupert, lived in an upscale (for the time and place) house designed and built by him. The design feature was a wonderful tower-like study filled with drafting instruments, lodge sword/regalia, awards and countless books. He had been a contractor and several toolsheds were still filled with fascinating but rusting equipment of once considerable value.

Papu, William Henry Rupert, was a state senator, so my brothers and I each enjoyed the experience of living in an Indianapolis hotel, one at a time, and serving as pages in the Indiana State Senate. My appointments came in three different sessions, but the most memorable was with Edward Jenner, later a U.S. senator, when he was virtually the only Republican voice in the Indiana legislature. At least, he was the loudest, shouting out his lonely NAY to almost every vote. Although I was only about ten years old, I was embarrassed by his antics in the mostly dignified chamber. However, he frequently sent me out for his cigar and my candy bar, which gave me the opportunity to explore different routes. I wandered through the displays of civil war flags, guns and such marvels as the stuffed carcass of the largest hog ever known, much impressed by the magnified echoes of my small shoes in the marble canyons. In those days, we wore steel plates on our heels to preserve the precious shoe leather, and even teachers and librarians understood the economic necessity for the clatter.

Grandmother Rupert was very much the grande dame of Bee Ridge, surrounded by her Downing kin, mostly prosperous farmers, and she more than compensated for the quiet modesty of the senator.

Both were self-educated, but saw to it that Mother and Aunt Helen were among the first from the area to attend college.

Senator Rupert

Granddad Evans' home, while slightly smaller, also was largely self-built and was perched on a hill offering exciting rides on all kinds of makeshift vehicles. There were goats, exotic birds, a pond with ducks and swans, abandoned coal mines along the rarely used Pea Vine Railroad track, and even a genuine operating one room school just waiting to be desecrated by the hellions visiting the neighborhood.

Like Papu, Granddad was highly intelligent and well read, though largely self taught. The resemblance ended there. Papu was a conservative member of the more liberal Democratic Party, while Granddad Evans was a radical Republican.

Granddad was always on the verge of economic success, rising to foreman status in a buggy and wheel works, then as engineer in a clay

10

factory in Terre Haute, Indiana. However, he lost much of his right hand in the steam engine, and spent the rest of his life in part time sales and a series of ill-fated entrepreneurial schemes.

Grandmother Evans was quiet, self-effacing and long suffering in support of her husband. He frequently embarrassed the family, especially Grandmother Rupert, with his vocal support of such causes as the Townsend Plan – TWO CHICKENS IN EVERY POT – TWO CARS IN EVERY GARAGE. This sounded crazy to most, but a very recent Republican president used similar pump priming logic to sell massive deficits, turning on its head the old meaning of "Conservative."

My boyhood trips to Bee Ridge were at the end of an age of many wonderful makes of automobiles, which were quickly being replaced by the Big Three. Ours was a plebeian model T, then a model A Ford, but Papu drove an air cooled Franklin until the engine fell out while he was driving on U.S. 40. Granddad had the marvelous high Essex with flower holders and even a spotlight.

At the age of thirteen, Dad ended his schooling to go to work in a brick factory, then a coal mine. He helped to keep his younger brothers in school-Howard to become dean of the college of education at Akron University, and Robert, a Methodist minister. This sacrifice fired Dad with a desire and respect for education which was not lost on his four sons. Through the midnight correspondence courses, he ground out a high school diploma by age thirty-five, and graduated from college at fifty-two, in the very month when I received my degree. The same spirit caused him to enroll Rupert in college at a time when savings were zero and total family income was about $100 per month. After Dad and four sons were finally educated, including two doctorates, mother cemented the tradition by completing her degree at age sixty, returning to teaching, and immediately starting work toward a graduate degree.

CHAPTER TWO – LOOK AT THEM EYES!

On very short notice, we held a family meeting, pooled our savings (twelve dollars in my case) and moved due East, right up U.S. 40 through Brazil and on to Plainfield, Indiana.

Despite Dad's arch Republican upbringing, Senator Rupert had been able to cash political chips, earned by his record of high esteem and low personal gain, to help his son-in-law obtain a scarce teaching appointment in the Indiana State Boys School (Reformatory). It was a difficult job, trying to get through to young thugs like alumnus John Dillinger, the infamous bank robber, but it brought security. Millions would have killed for such an opportunity during the Depression. In hindsight, this break for the family has hard-edged irony. My own career was holier-than-thou in refusing to allow family even the slightest appearance of privilege based on my positions or connections.

We were proud of Dad's new position and certainly had no intention of jeopardizing it, but we managed to do exactly that. In the woods between Plainfield and "the crick," we built the inevitable tree house and caves – simply trenches which were then covered with old tin and dirt. After crawling into the darkness, it was easy to believe that you were in the bowels of planet earth. One day as the club filed into the cave on all fours, the lead man with a flashlight scooted backwards, shouting "look at them eyes!" From a safe distance, we decided to smoke out the bear or whatever it was. A fire at the mouth of the cave had the desired effect, and out came the monster with four eyes – a tiny bespectacled boy in a dirty uniform – an escapee from the reformatory who had stumbled upon this convenient hideout. A club member living nearby brought his parents while the rest of us surrounded the escapee with sticks and a jackknife. His pathetic appearance lead the adults to swallow his story of mistreatment at the reformatory. They fed him for two or three days before he was recaptured, but the names which registered with the officials were those of the by-standing Evans boys. The incident was extremely embarrassing to Dad, just becoming well settled in his new position, and we were vastly relieved when he was not fired.

Plainfield had a swimming pool, but few children at that time had the necessary five cents, so The Crick by the Woods provided the town swimming hole. The diving platform was the end of the town sewer, which may help explain why I never became comfortable in water. In college, when facing a mandatory swimming test, I was reassured by the instructor that, at worst, I could float and paddle. "Anyone can float!" Twelve weeks later, he revised his theory to "almost anyone can float."

Having previously lived in the Crossroads of America, I could scarcely believe my good luck in moving to Plainfield with another wonder-of-the-world – The Van Buren Elm. A bronze plaque on this great tree commemorated the capsizing of the presidential carriage in the mud, leading the president to swear in general and avow in particular that this great nation would have a system of decent roads. One of the first was U.S. 40, known as the National Road, which seemed to appear everywhere in my boyhood. The "accident" was engineered by local rowdies in retribution for a Van-Buren veto of a highway bill, but he still took credit for ensuing improvements of the system.

At age seven, I sampled the antithetical careers of honest labor and crime. At four a.m. each summer morning, I would fumble off the alarm and stumble sleepily across town to the fields of cultivated gladiolas. While the florist was cutting the flowers, I would bundle them in my arms, becoming miserably wet and cold – for the wage of five cents per morning. (Enough to buy a huge quarter-pound candy bar). I felt proud and fortunate to have had this first paying job, but it was seasonal.

Again unemployed, I saw the great prize – a pearl handled pen knife in the five-and-dime store. For many days running, I had given the knife my daily devotion, so it required no great insight for the manager to determine that I had given in to temptation. Before he

14

confronted me, I had panicked and thrust the knife far up into a cast-iron public water pump. The manager did a masterful job of impressing me with the seriousness of the matter, including the probable effect on my mother if she were to learn. He certainly convinced me that crime does not pay, then offered to forget the matter if I returned the knife. This was impossible, but brother Allen saved me, as he did more than once, with a loan of twenty-five cents.

In those days, boys were raised with guns, so Rupert talked Dad into a .22 rifle. Naturally, we had to try our marksmanship on the insulators along the interurban rail line to Indianapolis. Countless shots somehow avoided cutting the power lines, so we tired of this sport. We came out into a clearing which we declared to be an abandoned homestead. Rupert decided that the most promising target was a red barrel beside a garage. Providentially, the garage housed neither automobiles nor living things.

On the next day, a neighbor boy told Rupert he thought our uncle was looking for us at the hotel. Without questioning why an uncle would not come to the house, Rupert hurried down to see which of several possible uncles it might be. The man had inquired about town as to the likely owners of a new rifle and had quickly stumbled onto the guilty parties. After some shouting, threatening and mediation, it was agreed that the rifle would be put away for the many months in which Rupert would be paying for the lost gasoline, barrel, and broken windows. This seemed unfair to Rupert because Allen and I had at least tried to hit the same target, but he was the only one with a paying job (printer's devil). I've forgotten Allen's excuse, but my token allowance was thoroughly committed to restitution for a window in the right field of our alley baseball diamond.

Despite this painful lesson, many additional bullets were fired into the air before we fully realized that each eventually returned to Earth with considerable penetrating power. We arranged a slightly safer firing range in our basement for the rifle and a homemade cannon which Dad bored from a truck axle. He intended the cannon strictly as a noisemaker, but we learned that black powder could propel a ball

15

bearing through a plank and well into the concrete basement wall. Like so many of our experiments, this ended in near disaster. Allen was sitting with the sack of powder between his legs when a spark flew back from the touchhole of the gun. He was immediately lacking eyebrows, eyelashes and most of his hair. His shocking appearance had a quieting effect on the whole neighborhood for months.

We also learned to make a respectable noise by crimping several heads from kitchen matches into an empty copper shell casing, then hitting the finished product with a heavy hammer. To this day, I carry a piece of copper in the knuckle of my left middle finger because we were afraid to tell our parents about this stupid trick.

It could have been worse, because one of my brothers had been trying to start a chain reaction by shooting down between his feet at a rifle cartridge packed in clay on the cap of a shotgun shell imbedded in the ground. Several years later, I was still curious about such matters. From about twenty-five feet, I used a .22 rifle to explode World War I blank Springfield ammunition stuck into woodpecker holes. Most of my shots missed, but one just creased the cartridge head, setting off a burning reaction instead of exploding. It took off like a rocket, and I looked down to see the brass casing protruding from my kneecap.

Stupid learns slowly. With my knee still bandaged, I switched targets to Lincoln pennies. Another freak shot clipped the edge of a coin and sent it zipping directly back at me. For several hours, my forehead bore the red, then blue bust of Abraham Lincoln.

Mother always drilled into us the idea that although we had little money, we were blessed with good minds and good family. In retrospect, however, I wonder if any of our moves between rented houses came at the request of the landlord because of the three boys. Perhaps our neighbor never knew that we shot a bird sitting on his roof. Perhaps others did not really object to the fact that I raised a flock of chickens in the middle of town. This was my first business venture and a source of great pride and useful cash as I sold fryers and eggs about the town. Just as I had thinned the flock down to nearly 100 percent daily egg production, either professional chicken thieves or neighbors made off with the entire flock. They apparently chloroformed and dognapped our faithful Pal, because he limped in days later with bleeding paws.

It was such a relief to have Pal back that I forgot my financial ruin. This noble mongrel was well known throughout central Indiana because of his travel mode. He started by riding in the protected valley between the right front fender and the hood, but as he grew bolder, he moved forward until he stood with front paws on the bumper of the car. On one trip, we lost him in a state park nearly 100 miles from home and finally conceded that he was lost. Once again, he appeared after several days, footsore but deliriously happy.

Previously mentioned were Plainfield's claims to fame – The Van Buren Elm and John Dillinger. For my seventh birthday, I traveled alone by bus to the 1933 Chicago World's Fair, staying with cousin Al Porcelli. Federal agents received a tip that Dillinger was in a theatre not far from the Porcelli home. When the show ended, he walked into a blizzard of gunfire. For many years, I treasured a chip from a power pole splintered by lead intended for public enemy number one. I heard later that the pole had to be replaced because so many chips were taken – then sold for fifty cents each.

The fair surely was spectacular. Al asked me to wait outside the famous Sally Rand fan dance venue, but made up for it with cotton candy, snow cones and a penny rolled out to a thin medallion. We returned late at night on the elevated train, which made an emergency stop for a man with a knife protruding from his chest. Back in the apartment, Al calmed our nerves with his treasured, though low fidelity, recordings of Verdi operas. He became one of the world's great Verdi fans, making many pilgrimages to Italy. After each performance of the Chicago Lyric Opera, we received the printed program lined with worshipful annotations.

We were all surprised (especially Mother) by an addition to the family – Philip Roland Evans. I took on my first real responsibility as babysitter or assistant mother to help with the considerable burden of the household.

CHAPTER THREE – HOME OF THE HOT DOGS

Those who think they know everything are a constant source of irritation to those of us who do.

By 1937, Dad was a bit tired of being called from bed to hunt escapees. He was delighted to accept a teaching position in the non-political (he assumed) atmosphere of a respected high-school, teaching eager and respectful students (he hoped). We moved to Frankfort, Indiana, in the middle of the school term. The boy assigned to help me become acquainted in the fifth grade pointed out his girlfriend and warned me that she was not available. Naturally, that made me take interest, and she found me novel, so we spent the next several years in a kind of relationship. Her role at that age was flirt/tease, and mine was fetch/carry. During most of this time, she towered over me and outweighed me by a good deal, but she was the belle of the class. Bob, the rejected one, was a scrappy little bulldog, and was downright disagreeable for a while. I was a bit taller, but considerably skinnier, so I was surprised that when I called his bluff on the playground one day, he backed down. We became fairly good friends but after he took up the sport of weightlifting and added thirty pounds of muscle, he savored my admission that I would not be looking to tangle with him.

Not long after arriving at the Lincoln School, I founded a newspaper, writing burning editorials, conducting a poetry contest with a prize of twenty-five cents, messing up the faculty room with my operation of the mimeograph and racking up enough profit to buy furniture for the room. I had sized up the principal as being a rather simple farm boy grown up, but when I realized what he had talked me into buying with the newspaper receipts, I knew that I had underestimated him.

Despite my chutzpah, it is doubtful that the community paid much attention to the arrival of the Evans family. Frankfort High School had just become the basketball power in a basketball crazy state. Our championship team that year had three players who later became college all Americans. Dad earned about $1,000 as a teacher, the principal $3,000, the superintendent $4,000 and the basketball coach $5,000. Only Coach Case was considered to be underpaid, and that must have been true, because North Carolina State soon paid well for his services.

Dad had never enjoyed paying rent, so when he had saved a few dollars for a down payment, he bought a place in the country. At $1,200, it was not much to look at. The entire plumbing system consisted of an outdoor two-hand pump – the kind you had to prime for what seemed like hours before the gurgle became a stream. The outdoor toilet seat was frequently covered with frost and the toilet paper roll almost invariably was down to the cardboard. We learned to go and leave as quickly as possible, trying to crumple the slick pages of a Sears Roebuck catalog into acceptable toilet paper.

Over the next few years, we painted, patched, hacked underbrush, broke ground for a seemingly huge garden and then started the real projects which Dad had in mind. We enlarged the basement and started a bathroom – excavating with a shovel and bucket. That was not hard enough work, so with chisel and sledgehammer, we attacked the bedrock which had been the reason for an undersized basement in the first place. I was honored to hold the chisel, but remember vividly my certainty that Allen eventually would damage more than my battered hands.

Granddad Evans visited us and proved that an aging man could still outwork three boys. With his help, we finally mixed concrete the hard way – in a wheelbarrow.

After a hard day of work, he could still show off his excellent physical condition for a man of sixty-plus by doing a one-legged deep knee bend. On his way home, he drove into the path of a truck and was severely injured. Mother and Dad scraped deep to help pay the hospital bill, and I have the impression that Granddad never fully recovered, dying while still in his sixties.

Two more wells were driven and an electric pump installed. The last well was costly. While the entire family was straining to pull up the stubborn old well point, our makeshift lever slipped and Mother was under the pile with a broken arm.

The finished lawn inched its way down the slope which even Dad admitted was impossible to cultivate for more garden, and the steepest section became a beautiful rock garden adorned by a silvered cannonball which will be explained later.

Livestock came and went. The sow was finally bred at some inconvenience both to herself and to those who had to transport her. Then she ate her own piglets, which we thought both unmotherly and gross. We tried a milk goat, but no one could stand to drink the milk on those occasions when there was any left after she finished kicking the bucket. She was finally butchered, but the meat was even less desirable. Allen got along well with several hives of bees, but the nasty critters sensed my dislike and stung me at every opportunity.

Despite his reluctant child laborers, Dad was much better at gardening than animal husbandry. He always had at least a half-acre in vegetables, but while hoeing weeds, it seemed to us more like forty acres. Mother filled the cellar shelves with canned goods and packed eggs in huge crocks of sodium silicate beside other crocks of sauerkraut. This may have contributed to her magical economics in feeding the family for a few dollars per week.

Although we griped a bit about the few chores expected of us, we were more concerned with the distance from town. When walking home on a dark night, the mile and a half seemed much farther. In the weather extremes of Indiana, and during the long introspective interludes, it sometimes felt like 150 miles. I was convinced that my friends in town regarded me as a country hick, and that my friends in the country considered me stuck up for going to school in town. Getting my own bicycle was an improvement, but riding home at night was thrilling, especially on the loose gravel of a downhill curve just before a narrow bridge, where I wanted to maintain speed to help in climbing the hill to the house. After leaving town, when there was no

21

moonlight, I judged my position on or off the road strictly by sound. Miraculously, my brothers and I made this trip hundreds of times without serious accident.

Even with the outhouse and other deficiencies, it was a good place to raise four boys. We built tree-houses, trapped muskrats (and a weasel which bit through my hand after playing possum), generally shot up the woods, and tracked rabbits in the snow. We could fire our arsenal of guns with only limited danger to the rest of Indiana. I was nearly carried away during my phase of making time bombs of sodium metal and calcium carbide in horse capsules dropped into closed containers with a little water. I probably should credit Allen with the idea, because he was my trail breaker in all kinds of chemical mischief. The upper floor of our high school was an easy toss from Prairie Creek, so we threw test bomblets out of the windows. Allen achieved brief hero status plus a trip to the office when he planted another explosive, I believe nitrogen tri-iodide, in the grade book of a science teacher who was providentially very good natured. The mixture dried to the desired state of instability by the end of the period, Mr. Swearingen closed his book, and it blew back open to wild applause.

Our largest carbide bomb was a fifty-five gallon drum long abandoned in the woods. Numerous people reported a strange clap of thunder right out of a clear blue sky. The piece de resistance was to be a large steel septic tank which had been left among the willows by a flood, but I could never remove the rusted cap. That was fortunate, I suspect.

Other assets of the neighborhood included a mixed up clan rivaling the fabled Jukes and Kalikaks, a neighboring barn with a basketball hoop, and a lovely stink factory. It rendered fat and bonemeal from dead animals, producing the kind of feed which now is blamed for the epidemic of mad cow disease. On a humid night with the right breeze, the half mile separating us from the plant was as nothing, but the real estate agent forgot to mention the odor when Dad was shopping for real estate.

Mother directed the Lincoln School Mother Singers in lieu of the sixty dollar tuition for me to attend school in Frankfort. Without this barter, I would have been forced to attend the Scroggy School, the neighborhood elementary school in our township. There were and are good one room schools, but this was not a good one. On the other hand, Lincoln School had one of the toughest, crustiest, best English teachers within my experience – the first to put me in my place and the first to really challenge me. During one school year, I read something like 140 books just to earn her praise as the most prolific reader. I thought that I was clever by quickly scanning much of this reading, but I realized later that she both knew and approved of my speed reading, which would be invaluable in attacking the mountains of books yet to come.

When I entered our five year high school in eighth grade, things began to happen. I was still small, but learning was easy, so I developed large ideas. At the slightest excuse, I would ask for a hall pass and would bypass the nearest restrooms in order to stroll through the wonderful tunnel. (The main buildings were separated by a state highway, so they were connected by a pedestrian tunnel.) It took nearly two years for me to tire of this extra mileage.

My experience with Senator Jenner convinced me that I could not do much worse as a politician, so I decided to run as eighth grade representative for the student council. Rupert had been a printer's devil for several years, so he stopped ignoring me long enough to print some posters, "no cigars or dollar bills – just my pledge of faithful service. Byron "Little Doc" Evans for student council." For no apparent reason, Dad had been known in several places at different times as Doc Evans. Rupert had inherited the title, and some of the older students called me "Little Doc." The formula and the printing were good enough to produce a landslide in my first political venture.

Not all of my activities that year were wholesome. The pheasant hunting season was very short, and we were distressed to learn that the opening came on a school day. Nevertheless, we probably would have resigned ourselves to this fate had it not been for a pronouncement by

"Doc" Evans, Teacher

our blustering little politician-principal to the effect that absolutely, finally, definitely, any students who skipped school to go hunting on opening day would be expelled if not executed. This became a major challenge, so both Allen and I were among the many missing. Allen pushed his luck still further by sporting a fresh pheasant tail feather. Nothing was ever said or done, but it must have been one additional embarrassment for Dad.

Soon after hunting season, the customary Christmas exchange brought me to a new low in behavior. For several years, the alphabetical location of my last initial had seated me next to a large, dull and homely girl of questionable parentage and fragrance. This prompted considerable ribbing from my friends, and I took it out on the poor girl. My gift to her was a baby bottle and a pair of rubber pants. She threw the bottle at my head, but I ducked in time to allow it to smash against the wall. Our too-meek teacher was speechless. The girl's big brother was not so meek. He was a giant, over-aged for high-school, and very tough, so I could have been maimed or killed. Instead, he backed Dad against the wall and demanded to know what was going to be done. To my immature classmates, I was a hero, but it turned out to be quite sobering to me. Ironically, that year I was awarded the American Legion medal for outstanding citizenship. Nearly sixty years later, when I finally attended a class reunion, I really wanted to apologize. Not surprisingly, Dorothy was among the missing, and there was no phone listing for her or the brother. No one even remembered them except me, and I suppose that was my punishment.

Some of the Frankfort Legionnaires would be disappointed to learn that I never joined their organization, because they were quite generous to me. Two years later, they sponsored my attendance at Indiana boys state, where I was elected chief justice of the Supreme Court and helped engineer the election of the governor. It was in the Legion home that I attended my lone Court of Honor to become a second-class Boy Scout (never passing the swimming requirement for first class). It also was the scene of my Girl Scout court of dishonor. A sometimes wild friend talked me into taking Dad's car out to the girl Scout camp so that he could visit his steady. I saw nothing wrong with it, so I drove right into the camp area and we walked up the hill to where the tents were located. I waited outside the tent and was enjoying the giggling until things began to pop. One of the Scout leaders chased Charley down the hill, waving a huge flashlight and screaming demands that he stop at once. He was not about to stop, and when he reached the car, he jumped into the driver's seat and tried to drive around her to the exit. She smashed the door glass with her flashlight. At that point I ran up to surrender for both of us, and we were in the soup. After public disgrace and private humiliation before the high tribunal, we were assured that it was only because of our outstanding previous record that we were not sent to prison or worse. In the unjust chauvinism of the time, the men probably thought it was funny, and the women took it more seriously.

My previous record was checkered, but Charlie's was terrible, and did not get better. He was bright and had everything he could want excepting normal parental attention. He finally was sent away to Culver Military Academy, then encouraged to try a third rate school in Tennessee, where he took great pleasure in making life miserable for the school officials, hoping he might be sent home. While home on furlough, he bragged about the various tricks he had taught and learned from other spoiled "inmates." He had a pocket full of expensive wristwatches. If there was anything he didn't need, it was money or another wristwatch, but he took both to show his contempt for authority. When he showed me his collection, I recalled with dismay that several months earlier, he had insisted on giving me a rather expensive watch. If he had not gone away to school, he might have helped me become a first class bum. On the other hand, perhaps I helped him settle down just a bit. The one place where we got along well and harmlessly was at the tennis court. We became junior city doubles champions, and this compensated for personality differences in prolonging our friendship. It also demonstrated that a strong partner would carry me farther than I could go alone, and I have applied this principle with great benefit in marriage as well as tennis.

There was another memorable furlough with Charlie. I had somehow been tapped to hold one of the coveted positions as soda jerk in the campus hang-out. Of about ten dollars in cash received on Saturday night for the week's work, eight dollars was spent in a Sunday afternoon flying lesson. The cow pasture airport was appropriately located near a cemetery, because it was responsible for several deaths (power lines at one end and a creek cutting across the center). On my sixteenth birthday, I completed the required eight hours of dual instruction and made my first solo flight, having already passed the physical despite problems with color perception. The solo was uneventful except that I came in a bit high over the creek, killed the engine, preventing another pass, and ground looped when I saw that I was running out of pasture.

26

Charlie was thrilled to learn that he was the buddy of such a young pilot and insisted on taking a ride. My license, unbelievably, was good for life, but strictly limited to solo flying until I logged thirty-two more hours and passed a much more difficult exam. However, I found it impossible to refuse both Charlie's flattery and his offer to pay the plane rental. We agreed that I would pick him up in a cornfield about half a mile from my home. Shortly after he parked his uncle's car by the field, I landed the sixty-five horsepower Piper Cub without incident. By the time we took off over the barn, the farmer had run outside to have a look, and a couple of cars stopped. When we returned from our joy ride, which featured a very sloppy inside loop I had taught myself from the Civil Air Patrol manual, the word had spread and it looked like the multitudes waiting to welcome Lindbergh. The attention was heady, but I feared at least one of the garlands awaiting me might be made of hemp. Instead of the planned landing pattern, I turned for the open countryside. Charlie protested that his borrowed car was back at the edge of town, but I saw an attractive field of corn stubble and deposited him there to get back the best he could. I headed back to the airport as quickly as possible, and was not surprised to see the manager waiting for me. He asked if I had any trouble, and I assured him that everything was fine. He pointed to a six-foot-long. corn stalk dragging from the rear wheel. I left without comment, but with tail between my legs, and I never darkened that hangar door again.

I did resume flying after the war, and earned the private pilot rating to carry passengers. In this stage, I flew from large and well equipped airports, but my last flight was from another

Peg's Only Flight With Me

27

cow pasture, and was nearly as much of a debacle. When a high school friend came to visit her, Peggy decided the most impressive way to show off the Oregon mountains was from the air. We rented an Aeronca and nonchalantly took off without bothering to verify the(defective) wind indicator with as much as a wet finger. I finally realized that we were taking off downwind when the barely adequate field kept getting shorter and shorter, and the fence kept getting higher and higher. We cleared the fence by sheer will power and I never handled a plane again until a VIP junket to Pensacola Naval Air Station many years later.

Not Quite Davis Cup

Except for my tennis, church league basketball and some distance running by Allen, the Evans boys were not athletes in high school. However, Allen managed to raise our whole level of respect in just a few seconds one afternoon. He had been appointed hall monitor, much against his will, but having been given the responsibility, he was certainly going to do the job. He served a detention summons on the school's beefiest football tackle, who stuffed it in Allen's pocket with a shove and received a right to the nose which left him sitting on the ground blinking. There was some speculation about town and in the family as to whether the slender Evans boy may have landed a lucky punch, but there was enough doubt that big John decided to take his detention without a second round.

Time and again, we were anything but a help to Dad in his position, but I suspect that he secretly enjoyed some of our scrapes because of his own restricted boyhood and his total lack of respect for the principal who was flustered and ambivalent concerning some of our actions.

With my lack of athletic confidence, I was frankly surprised when I was picked from a summer softball league to play in an All-Star Game against a visiting team of girl professionals. Naturally, they had a windmill pitcher with blazing speed, and while they trounced us, I managed to get one of the only two hits for our team. If pressed, I probably would have admitted to a lucky swing, but I do have a relatively fast reaction time.

However, a quick reaction was no help in later years, during my other two auditions for the role of idiot: donkey basketball and "real" basketball against the Harlem Globetrotters second string. The former probably contributed to my present ugly CAT scans, while the latter thoroughly erased my illusions of basketball stardom.

The hangout known as Aughe Brothers Drugs had a prime location on the courthouse square near the high school. The soda fountain grossed big money for its time, but the profit was low because of the way that we robbed poor Harry, the owner. The soda jerks were good students and leaders, but what a bunch of characters and perverted geniuses! Frank became the town's leading physician. Greasy (also known as "double duty") surprised everyone by becoming high school principal, then superintendent in the town where he had been chief clown. Then there was Doc, graduated from Little Doc.

For about two years, the drug store was virtually my home. We were paid seventeen cents per hour and all we could eat/give away. Our friends were rewarded with the largest, richest concoctions we could devise. Our enemies might find anything from sal hepatica to dishwater in their milkshakes. When serving customers on the other side of the store, we were all business, but the soda fountain was non-stop comedy theater. It is questionable whether anyone else appreciated it, but we entertained each other royally. Frank's favorite ice cream customer was a little old lady who came in every Saturday morning. She always took the farthest table, invariably wrapped in a long muffler even in summer. Frank would walk to the back of the store and inquire politely as to her wish.

"Cream," was the standard order.

"What kind of cream?"

"Plain cream."

"And how much cream would you like?"

"Ten cents."

Frank would give a half-bow and return to the soda fountain to complete the ritual. While the other soda jerks and the kids on the bar stools howled with delight, he would solemnly reach into the refrigerator for a bottle of cream, pour some in a saucer, then set it aside and serve the lady her dish of vanilla ice cream. Frank was a natural comic, but was sensitive to the feelings of others. His formal treatment made the poor old girl feel very important, blissfully ignorant as to the source of the merriment at the fountain. She regarded Frank as the perfect gentleman.

This may sound like a slip into fiction, but trust me: the first time I ever saw Peggy, now my wife of almost sixty years, was at the soda fountain. Impressed by her fresh beauty, I announced to the other jerks that she was mine and asked whether anyone knew her. She was identified as Peggy Irwin, of Jackson Township High School. Although she lived less than five miles away, I was not to meet her until more than a year later when we were both attending Purdue.

Like most clowns and other teenagers, we talked big, but were individually pretty shy concerning girls. To screen our uncertainty, we kept up a constant stream of thinly veiled off color chatter. One recurrent topic was Spanish Fly, called cantharides by the pharmacists on the other side of the store. It was an old time blistering agent rumored to make the female of any species amorous toward any part of anything resembling a male of any species. Our school buddies did not know what to hope for or fear when we threatened to lace their food. Fortunately, as dumb as we sometimes appeared, we did have sense enough not to tamper with any drugs. Alcohol was something we had to try, but it was not that accessible or affordable. When Charlie filched a bottle of apricot brandy from his father, I demonstrated my ability to do head flips on a concrete sidewalk. Charlie surprised me by being the one in the group to remain cold sober. Despite his other vices, he had seen the ill effects of his father's drinking, so on this occasion he turned out to be my guardian. I had no other drinking incidents until I later tried to prove my manhood as a fraternity pledge. The tumbler of bourbon which I drained could have killed me, but I only wished to die during a few minutes of violent regurgitation.

Our crew headed to Indianapolis one evening for the Circle Theater and a look at the spectacular monuments of the city. It was early in World War Two, and we were unbelievably honored when a beribboned Air Corps major asked if we knew where he could sleep, since the hotels were full. Having a huge room with two beds and a sofa, we invited him to share our quarters. On our way home after a long and tense night, we compared notes and agreed that our hairy hero was a homo.

During my term as president of the junior class, I carried the major responsibility for two major business operations of the student body. The prom came off quite well. We had the armory sufficiently filled to pay for the band and extravagant decorations, and still leave money in the bank for the partying of the senior year, which I missed completely.

The other big deal was the ordering of class sweaters. We selected maroon-and-something for our colors, which may have been rather ugly, though this is not the point to be made here. My sense of loyalty to the drug store, whose profits I gave away daily, led me to have it selected as official supplier of the sweaters. This was not as far-fetched as it sounds, because the drug store did a fair business in athletic

31

goods, including some sweaters. The disturbing element in hindsight (and I had no clue at the time) was that not one person in the school or community pointed out to me that I just might have a conflict of interest. Perhaps in our small town code of business ethics, it was expected. The only serious question from the soda jerks was why Dick Aughe, virtual co-manager with his father, had the privilege of measuring all the girls' chests when he already had a young and beautiful wife. (Question from the soda fountain,"Where would you rather be than deep in the heart of Texas?" Choral response: "- - - - - - - - - Virginia.") Dick was athletic and could have mopped the floor with all of us, or fired us, but he would laugh it off and merely twist the nearest ear.

Pushing My Luck With The Boss

Frank and Greasy were the ringleaders of the soda jerks, but I was less careful about hiding my excesses on behalf of my buddies. About six months after he should have thrown me out, Harry called me up to his desk overlooking the main floor."Is something bothering you, Doc?" This gruff, but fatherly observation was the understatement of

32

that decade. I could only feel thoroughly ashamed of my "work," agree with the unstated volumes of indictment and offer to step down a month earlier than I had planned. So ended my first regular job, which taught me how to work long hours, then get on my bicycle for an endless ride home late at night. (I also learned that when drying dishes, if one slipped out of my hands, I could break its fall with my foot and usually save it – except when I drop-kicked it clear across the store. Even today, I use that reflex when I drop anything.)

CHAPTER FOUR – I BEEN WORKIN' ON DE RAILROAD

That summer, when I turned sixteen, my wages increased by about 1000 percent. Fred Whitmore, one of my more wholesome friends, was the son of a middle echelon executive of the Nickel Plate Railroad. It was time for Fred's baptism into the industry, and he was allowed to bring along a friend. We were assigned to a bridge crew, which was the SWAT team of railroad repair, subject to middle-of-the-night deployment for bridge washouts, derailments and other emergencies. This resulted in considerable overtime pay, so the jobs were highly desirable to adults, let alone green high school kids. Obviously, the rest of the crew, who had earned their assignments the hard way, were going to make us prove ourselves, while being outwardly supportive of the son of a big boss.

Fortunately, Freddie was a hard worker, determined to make his mark, and I wasn't about to be left behind. There was one difference: he was a three-sport varsity athlete, smallish but hard as nails. In those first weeks of swinging sledgehammers, carrying timbers and other new tests, Fred's muscles ached, so you can imagine how mine felt. We showed the hard-bitten old timers that we could stick with them through an around-the-clock flood repair crisis, so they began to concede that the babies were all right. Wartime freight was heavy and the labor supply was tight; the standard day was twelve hours, with a few lasting as long as seventy-two hours.

We asked no sympathy for our blisters, and received none for our sunburn when foolish enough to work without shirts. However, I received much attention when laid up in the bunk car for three days with creosote burns received while working with a pile driver. Any of the men could have told me that my job of guiding the treated timbers under the pile driver head required heavy clothing, but they decided to let me find out the hard way. Throughout two long nights, my upper body throbbed with every tick of the courthouse clock, and our bunk car was nearly a mile from the clock.

Every railroad crew has its characters, but this was especially true in wartime. Many had come north from the hill country. The man across the aisle kept a length of rail iron under his bunk to use as a barbell for keeping fit. The next man kept a jug of genuine mountain dew to use as a bar in keeping unfit. He impressed us greatly, but not as a role model. After twelve hours of backbreaking work and a huge meal, most of us flopped on our bunks for the night. Rummy would drink alone for two or three hours, head for the cat houses, stumble home and sleep for three hours fully clothed, wash his face and start all over again. His name was Rumsfeld, but the nickname was fully earned by his hard drinking. He was the first of two drunks (five years apart) to throw a punch at me simply because they did not like my "shit-eatin'" grin. We were standing around kibitzing a poker game when I noticed him staring at me through his fog. Without a word or a hint, he threw a roundhouse which grazed my chin. I was so surprised that I did nothing and even more surprised when the foreman thanked me for holding my temper. He said that I easily could have killed the old drunk, and I suspect that some of the crew would have done exactly that. Later, Rummy apologized and told me he had no idea what got into him.

To help settle my nerves, Fred and I walked down the track to a bowling alley in Muncie, Indiana. I rolled a game of 266 – the highest of my life by far. The game started with eight strikes before the roof fell in with a pocket split.

Young men were scarce during the war. Fred and I were amazed one evening to see a group of well-dressed young people come up to knock on the bunk car door and invite us to a dance party on a houseboat on Lake Manitou. We were briefly suspicious of any group attracted by our appearance, but we quickly dressed and had a delightful evening despite the fact that I am not much of a dancer.

Beside learning the value of hard work and blisters (and the value of higher education to minimize future blisters), we developed at least

36

partial understanding of the scorn felt by laborers when a luxurious private car of a railroad official or a potentate of another corporation was placed alongside the bunk car. This experience surely helped Fred keep perspective when the shoe was on his other foot as vice president of a larger railroad. On weekends, we also learned that freight trains run more frequently than passenger trains, so we almost mastered the art (not used by me recently) of jumping from a moving caboose and tumbling down the embankment without losing, though once emptying, a suitcase.

The railroad did wonders for my meager college savings account. I had very briefly tried detasseling seed corn, and countless odd jobs which paid very little. Washing windows at the court house proved to be a never ending task and required the handling of great quantities of pigeon droppings. Forty years later, I was required to have a chest X-ray to renew my administrator's license. The public health officer said, "You kept a piece of shrapnel for a souvenir." Seeing my amazement, he pointed at a circular image in the X-ray. When I told him of my success in avoiding combat, he pointed to the scar on my chest directly in line with the "shrapnel." I realized that he was looking at an old chicken pox scar and finally convinced him that my only bullet holes were self inflicted. He then asked if I had ever been in a position to catch one of the diseases carried by pigeons. The X-ray was showing a pellet of calcium generated in my lung to isolate the damaged spot.

My window washing was interrupted by a happier assignment substituting for the elevator operator. Although not air-conditioned in those days, the old stone courthouse was much cooler inside than outside. I did not yet know him, but Peggy's father probably was a client for my vertical chauffeuring, because he was a Clinton County Commissioner.

Music is very important to me, yet I never mastered an instrument, and unlike Rupert, my singing voice did not make the grade for solo work. After mother's futile efforts to get us to practice the piano, I tried the bassoon, but we could not afford to buy one, and it was not easily borrowed and transported by bicycle.

My eventual solution to the musical dilemma of no practice-no music was the discovery of mechanical music. I am not referring to recordings, which we also enjoy, but to our collection of large antique music boxes. The ingenious designs (stemming from the watch makers of Switzerland), quality of materials, and patient craftsmanship allow these to keep producing their fascinating tunes after 150 to 200 years.

Living

The SARATOGIAN — Thursday, July 2, 1987

LOOK, NO HANDS — Dr. Byron Evans, left, and his wife Peggy listen to their 1929 Ampico player piano as it turns out a tune at their Saratoga Springs home. The baby grand piano is one of nearly 100 mechanical m... vices the Evanses have collected over the years.

(Staff photo by Bruce

Reproducing Grand

The star of the collection is a nine foot tall Dutch musical clock made about 1750. In addition to showing time by the second, minute,

38

hour, day of the week, day of the month, phase of the moon, sign of the zodiac, quarter strike, repeating strike to avoid the necessity of lighting a candle in order to learn time in the middle of the night, automaton figures moving with the music, it plays a short tune after the half hour strike and a longer tune after the hour strike. The six melodies are produced by a cylinder with thousands of tiny pins triggering hammers which strike fifteen solid silver bells.

Made by Pieter Rossignol in Rotterdam, the clock was a special order for the Dutch estate in Rye, N.Y. which later became an amusement park. Family members carried the clock to Cleveland, Long Island, then Saratoga Springs. A friend and antique dealer purchased it from the Purdy estate . Knowing of my music boxes, the new owner brought the clock to me to replace the largely missing musical mechanism. I had to explain that these were one-of-a-kind, and the missing parts must be crafted from scratch. My disappointed friend later came back asking me to buy the clock for a little more than his investment. He had a terminal blood disease, so what could I do?

For the next ten years, I spent countless hours trying to find an affordable restoration, finally learning of an American-born resident of the Netherlands who specializes in exactly this kind of clock. His estimate was impressive, and he cautioned that costs could run beyond the estimate, but he seemed like an honest man. After three more years, he called to say that the job was finally finished at a cost midway between the original estimate and the amount I had feared. HOWEVER, his accountant advised against releasing the clock until he finally settled a three year battle with UPS International, which was a total shock and surprise to me. When I shipped the mechanism prepaid, UPS had demanded cash payment from the restorer for value added tax, and later billed him twice again for duplicate payments. He is an honest, naive craftsman, and he finally surrendered to their threat of legal action. The tax apparently was improper for a repair job to be returned to me, and the rate was triple the levy for antiques. UPS stonewalled his attempts to get a refund (finally returning one of his three payments) and would not even supply invoices detailing the charges. Not wanting more years to pass without seeing the clock, I sent additional funds to cover the craftsman.

He refused to make the return shipment by UPS, so we agreed on an old line Dutch company which was more expensive. The clock arrived with major damage, which the insurance company disavowed since the crate was intact. I protested that the craftsman had deliberately built a crate as strong as a safe. It must have been dropped a considerable distance to shear off the steel bolts fastening the music mechanism to the clock. They finally agreed to a partial payment for work by a New York craftsman since I was not about to ship overseas again.

Is the clock worth all of the grief? Not even if it were a prototype by Leonardo da Vinci, but it kept me off the streets for years and now gives me something to talk about.

In recent years, I have gained great relaxation and satisfaction from playing the piano and organ by ear. Years after our initial failures to accept the finest instruction at no cost, each of us had a slightly contemptuous short course from Mother. Today, it might be labeled, "Chords for Dummies." We must have been a colossal disappointment to this consummate musician, who played church organ and piano for more than eighty years. For each Sunday she missed, there must have been dozens of choir practises, funerals, concerts, etc.

My musical zenith was the restoration, with Peggy's forbearance, then full participation, of a 1929 Knabe/Ampico B reproducing grand piano. This was the last evolution of the early player piano which allegedly prompted the daughter of Lord Byron to co-postulate early computer theory (it was one of the first binary systems). Our piano was one of only a few made before the depression choked off production, but it was a wonderful design. The makers rented Carnegie Hall and hired Josef Hoffman, a great classical pianist of the day, to play one piano, then fake playing the other while it operated from a roll. The audience then voted their opinion as to which performance was live – the vote was almost exactly fifty-fifty.

I had answered an ad for a different reproducer (a piano pneumatically duplicating the exact expression used by the artist, unlike the plunkety-plunk of the commonly known upright players). After I agreed to the terms of the owner, he decided not to sell. While bemoaning this experience at a graduation party, I was told by Bill Dake, president of Stewarts' ice cream and convenience store chain, that he might be able to help. His Aunt Glad owned this instrument, which had not played except as a piano for twenty-five years, and she really wanted the Steinway owned by Bill's wife, A.C., who would really prefer a new spinet. We quickly agreed to buy a spinet, and took the reproducer in a three-way swap which delighted everyone. The Ampico B roll is unique, and there were no rolls with the piano, so we spent several years collecting rolls, some of which disintegrated at the first play.

For an entire winter, parts of the reproducer were scattered about our family room as Peggy replaced nearly 1000 feet of rubber tubing. I split open, re-covered and re-glued some ninety bellows of different sizes, rebuilt the vacuum pump, replaced motor mounts and deteriorated white metal fittings, opened, cleaned and lubricated all the valves, etc., etc. One slight problem – the only technical manual in print apparently was based on the prototype piano. When it went into production, the design was changed in a number of ways, but the manual was not updated. (Depression cost crisis?) Rupert saved the day by visiting my niche under the piano where I spent many hours with pillow, trouble light and manual. He has fantastic instinct and knowledge of electromechanical workings.

What a thrill when we finally reassembled the marvelous machine and it played on the first try!

For years, I would drag in from late night school board meetings all over the county, collapse and listen to Rachmaninoff play his own *C-sharp minor*, or Gershwin play his own *American in Paris* or *Rhapsody in Blue*, or Scott Joplin play his own ragtime. Then I would play live by ear for a few minutes, pretty badly, and would be totally relaxed and restored. After building a fine roll collection and enjoying the piano for more than twenty years, we were called by Bill Dake and asked if we would consider selling so he could give it to Aunt Glad's new home, Wesley Manor. The answer was sorry, but no, because I had said it would be the last of our treasures to go. Peggy once asked if she was factored into that statement, and I said, "Don't test me". After talking it over, we called Bill again and agreed to donate the piano if he would buy the roll collection and the beautiful inlaid cabinet and donate them. Aunt Glad did not live long after the transfer, but she did listen to many rolls and imagined that they were from her younger years.

Back to my mixed record in high school: a brief, but invaluable experience was my year on the debating team. The national topic that year was: Required Military Service For All Boys and Girls? We lost only to the team which went on to win the state championship. Debaters must be quickly reversible, because they may be assigned either side of the question. Whether for required service or agin it, my formal presentation always included a Wake Island scenario with a melodramatic monologue by a dying boy. By changing only a few words, I made it fit the side of the argument I was pleading at the moment. It worked a few times, but in the debate which really counted, I can still see the judges wincing. I learned the hard way that a few minutes spent in toning down the phony sentiment could have paid off handsomely. Still, debating was wonderful preparation for my lifetime of public speaking and pleading on behalf of education.

Dick Harrison, a debating teammate, and I had somehow learned that Purdue University had adopted a wartime provision for admission by examination prior to high school graduation. We passed the exam and then checked with our high school principal to see if we might still receive a diploma. All graduation requirements had been met early except for senior civics. We were told that if we took a college course in civics and waived college credit, we would be granted diplomas. Instead of wasting the college credit, we decided to gamble that college degrees should be worth more than a high-school diplomas. This has taken much explaining over the years when filling out applications, but the decision may have saved my life at the time when a magic number of college credits plucked me from the ranks of infantry combat replacements.

The Purdue summer session started immediately following our junior year exams, so there was little time to prepare for college. Dick and I both pledged Delta Tau Delta - perhaps because Rupert had been a Delt at Butler University and one of our friends from Frankfort was a member of the chapter. Besides, the Delt house was very conveniently located with respect to the College of Engineering. My room was envied by many of the brothers, because it had a separate entrance, but roommate Ed was not so choice. He had been a precocious young man, entering college at age fifteen. By eighteen, he had flunked many courses and had lost much of his hair-perhaps because of his debauchery. Many times, when returning from the library, I found myself locked out. We had no housemother, and Ed explained that he felt the need for someone to mother him.

Ours was the last pledge class to get the full hell week treatment. Some of the activities (mostly conducted in the nude) included ping pong, where we were the balls propelled by paddle over oak tables; toilet paper races – long strips of toilet paper were laid out on the floor for each pledge, and gobs of peanut butter, mustard and butter were spaced along the paper and liberally sprinkled with pepper. The last pledge to get the entire mess in his mouth was given the most generous paddling. We also played Minnesota shift and other games too crude to detail. After seven days of such indignities, we were required to assemble items requiring imagination and chutzpah. My assignment was a 100 pound cannonball from the courthouse square across the river. Cars were forbidden during hell week, so I was forced to use a city bus. The driver was patient until I nearly ripped off the step of the bus in rolling the cannonball out.

By the time I became pledge master for the next class, we were ordered by the fraternity national office to clean up hell week (this happens every few years, usually following the death of a pledge somewhere), but I believe I would have done so without prompting. Hell week, of course, is a rite of passage – good up to a point – but most sophomores simply do not have the judgment to know when to stop. Two of my pledge class brothers left the fraternity and the university in complete humiliation because of the excess. All of this came back in vivid detail when the Iraqi torture scandal surfaced. I had no doubt that some of the techniques were learned in a fraternity.

My financial backing for college was quite limited, so it was obvious that I would need to work. With more good luck than good planning, I stumbled onto a job chauffeuring a crippled lawyer who lived near the fraternity. This not only paid the bills, but it even provided a new car for occasional dating. More than either of these, he gave me an understanding of what can be accomplished by a person who is completely helpless except for his mind. I got up early to go to his house, carry him from bed to the toilet, then wait until he was dressed, shaved and ready for work. His incredible wife did everything for him except the lifting. Transferring him from the wheelchair to the car was tricky, but since I could not hold his dead weight at arm's length, I learned to swing/throw him into the passenger seat, sometimes losing his hat, but never quite fracturing his skull.

When I needed a quick twenty dollars, my ace in the hole was a case of cheap whisky which I had acquired. There were times when a fraternity brother was willing to pay outrageous prices for a bottle, even this bad stuff.

In the grooming of young fraternity men for campus politics, there were two key appointments at the end of freshman year. I was told that I was greatly honored to be elected to Skull and Crescent, but I knew that Hose Nose Easley was getting an even more prestigious appointment to the Green Potters. Therefore, he owed me a favor, and it was not long before I had a chance to use it. The nine to one ratio of men to women at Purdue (even in wartime) made it difficult to monopolize the date book of Peggy Irwin, the girl in the drug store. I had now been with her enough to feel absolutely certain of my first impression. She became our fraternity's nominee for Freshman Queen, and with the help of Hose Nose, she was elected one of the finalists. Tragically, her father was in a serious accident, and she withdrew from college before prom night when the decision and crowning would take place. From that time on, her priorities were her father's recovery and my education. She attended several different colleges while following my career and became well educated without the degree. She is a voracious reader, and has incredible recall of detail, mentally filing names by initial. On countless occasions, she has recalled the initial of an obscure name, at which point I can solve the puzzle.

We continued dating as commuters during my final weeks at Purdue, and my grade point average dropped from 5.3 to 3.5. That seemed unimportant since I was getting ready to go to war. By

Peg's Parents

carrying a heavy course load, I had nearly two years of credit from one summer and one school year. Expecting that I would be drafted upon turning eighteen in July, I decided to enlist in a branch of my choice. Despite my brief experience as a civilian pilot, the Air Force was out because of color blindness. As reported in chapter one, the Navy V-12 liked my test results, but turned down my physical exam because of the facial burns. I felt no bitterness toward the ensign who was reading the book, but thought it inconsiderate not to read me the book before I traveled to Chicago at my own expense.

This left the army, so I volunteered for early induction and went to work in a local factory while waiting for orders. Needing a goal for my earnings, I decided to buy Peggy an engagement ring. I pushed aside the safety guard on my punch press, and held down the foot treadle so

45

that I could feed a blank with every stroke of the twenty-ton head. On two occasions, small crescents appeared on the ends of a fingernail, but without a drop of blood. It was fortunate that I was a short term employee, in a non- union shop and known to be leaving for service, because I demolished the pay rates for piece work. In some shops, that could earn you broken kneecaps. Dangerous, but effective, my job produced a small Keepsake diamond ring costing $150 – a huge amount for me at that time.

In my last week of work, I was taken to lunch by the other Doc Evans. He and his father (same name and nickname) ran the local gambling room. I had received some interesting mail intended for him, but we had not met. He hinted at financial support for me to study mathematics of probability when I returned from service. I never took this seriously – what would it get me other than money?

CHAPTER FIVE – TAKE DOWN YOUR SERVICE FLAG, MOTHER, YOUR SON'S IN THE A S T P

On September 18th, 1944, I checked into Camp Atterbury for two weeks of screening for lice, literacy and venereal diseases, then shipped off to Fort Hood, Texas, by train. In the state with too much of everything, we settled down to the business of becoming so miserable that we would be delighted to go overseas. Appointed "acting gadget" over a squad including the very best and worst of our species, I soon earned a reputation of having more nerve than good sense by facing down "the stomper." Three years into the war, Texas was getting down to the dregs of its manpower, and I suspect that this older draftee was given a choice between prison and the infantry. He believed that the best introduction to an enemy (and every man was a potential enemy to him) was a vicious surprise attack, flooring him with a quick low body blow, then stomping his face and kidneys. Within two weeks, at least eight from our barracks had been victims, including Al Carlson, who became my college roommate and best man. When I saw the redneck building up steam for another attack, I simply told him that this time he would need to lick two of us. He turned red, swore a blue streak, and threatened to kill me, but stayed out of my way and attacked no one else, at least in our barracks. I was probably very lucky, because Al was in better shape than I was.

At the end of our training cycle, the battalion was split into two sections – one group to replace casualties in the Battle of the Bulge, and the other to equally impossible assignments at the beachhead on Okinawa. This meant going into the suicidal front line positions without the normal opportunity for seasoning, but we felt surprisingly little concern about our chances.

The last opportunity for reprieve was the list of special assignments for further training. One man was needed for the ski troops, and we had in our company a ski instructor with a family – a perfect match?

47

No. Personnel selected a boy from the south, and sent the experienced man to Okinawa. For the single opening in chemical warfare, they picked a high school graduate and sent a middle aged chemical engineer to Belgium. The remaining assignments were for engineering training through the army specialized training program (A S T P).

Early in the war, RPI President William Hotchkiss had proposed a college-based program to prevent the draft from decimating the national pool of technological talent. This was supported by most university presidents, who were concerned about keeping their institutions alive. Secretary of War Stimson accepted credit for the idea and gained the support of President Roosevelt and the powerful Republican Senator Robert Taft. Most line generals were lukewarm or antagonistic even though the comparable Navy V programs were running successfully. They grudgingly accepted the program, but during the first infantry manpower crisis (1943–44), an entire A S T P class was shipped out of the various colleges to Europe. It is hard to be objective but I have never understood how otherwise intelligent generals could have been so near sighted in cannibalizing technological potential when the Navy at that time was relatively rich with manpower.

Now Washington had decided that the engineering pipeline should be refilled with students with at least thirty-five and not more than forty-four semester hours of engineering credit. Several of us were ordered to Oregon State College in Corvallis, Oregon. We knew nothing about A S T P or O S C, but our elation betrayed the bravado which we had shown for our apparent roles as infantry replacements. Later, we learned that Andy Rooney, the curmudgeon of Sixty Minutes, Henry Kissinger, and New York City Mayor Ed Koch had been our comrades-in-slide-rules.

Our orders called for a tight train connection which we just missed, so we had an emergency overnight layover at an air force headquarters unit in downtown San Francisco. Having just come from field training, we found the beds and the meal menus so fabulous that we did not leave the building to see the city.

Back on the train, we soon found ourselves in the strangely green Willamette Valley, where Corvallis turned out to be a quiet little college town. Even though it was January, our hated overcoats were packed away and we could even stroll in the misty rain without raincoats.

Our accelerated program kept us running, but after basic training in Texas, it was wonderful to be back on a campus. Dating was not in my plan, so I jumped at an offer from the physical education department to teach tennis to recovering wounded veterans, though feeling guilty about accepting two dollars per hour. The extra cash was most welcome, and it gave me one more item to pad my limited resume.

Peggy Coed

Peggy jokes about my luring her away to Oregon, but my diary attests to a sacrificial letter urging her to return to Purdue as quickly as her father's recovery might permit. Instead, history shows that she began a campaign to return to college somewhere else.

After an initial "nothing doing," Peggy's parents consented to her crazy idea of attending Oregon State College for the spring quarter. I did not overburden myself with homework, and with one exception, we had a glorious time. Near the end of the quarter, I suffered serious burns from an exploding water jacket of a test engine, and Peggy developed a full blown case of poison oak. She made a flying trip back to Indiana, returning just in time for us to be married on my 19th

49

birthday, July 3rd, 1945. Young, indeed, but it was wartime and we rationalized that I was a college senior and remarkably mature! At least, the marriage has lasted almost sixty years.

Few will believe this, but the truth must be chronicled. Shortly before we married, I received a weekend pass, so we decided to see the big city of Portland. The desk clerk at the New Heathman Hotel misunderstood our intentions, although I had clearly indicated our different names. When we checked in, he sent us upstairs with the bellboy, who left us in a room with a double bed. We were so

Photo Carried Daily for Sixty Years

flabbergasted that we said nothing, but sat and looked at each other. Peggy ended up sleeping under the sheet and I was on top of the sheet. We returned to the same hotel for our honeymoon, and this time we were assigned a room with twin beds! The bill was $15.50 for three nights.

Yes, we each married a virgin, a condition almost as rare in 1945 as today. Though from a warm-blooded species, we have always been glad that we waited, but have no illusions of superiority over friends who chose otherwise. If strength of character was the major factor, it was mostly to the credit of Peggy. Her beauty and the predatory instincts of the mostly older boys who lined up for dates certainly made her a prime target. My defenses were multiple: later social development, being attracted only to the prettiest girls, huge respect for Peggy, and natural cowardice.

How better to tell my feelings for Peggy than Lord Byron's "She Walks in Beauty," written nearly 200 years ago?

> She walks in beauty, like the night
> Of cloudless climes and starry skies;
> And all that's best of dark and bright
> Meet in her aspect and her eyes:
> Thus mellow'd to that tender light
> Which heaven to gaudy day denies.
>
> One shade the more, one ray the less,
> Would half impair the nameless grace
> Which waves in every raven tress,
> Or softly lightens o'er her face;
> Where thoughts serenely sweet express
> How pure, how dear their dwelling-place.
>
> And on that cheek, and o'er that brow,
> So soft, so calm, yet eloquent,
> The smiles that win, the tints that glow,
> But tell of days in goodness spent,
> A mind at peace with all below,
> A heart whose love is innocent!

Chicken dinner for the entire wedding party cost a total of twenty-five dollars. Our families were a million miles away, so those present with us at the wedding were the Minister, best man Al Carlson, my other room mate, Earl Doubet, and their girls, bridesmaids Colleen Roberts and Margaret Funge.

Earl was forever bragging about Peoria and Caterpillar, and we did not have the mutual bond that I enjoyed with Al. However he suddenly came to mind some thirty-five years later when I needed to quickly equip a diesel shop with a very limited budget. I reasoned that Earl surely would have returned to his beloved Peoria, so I asked the operator to place a person to person call to him at the Caterpillar Corporation. My hunch was right on – he was President of Caterpillar International, and we soon had a brand new diesel test engine. The epilogue is almost as strange – when I followed with a friendly call only a couple of years later, the same office said they did not recognize the name.

July 3, 1945

Now that we were independent, Peggy went to the employment office and was told that our commandant, Colonel Webster, needed a secretary. The employment counselor suggested that she allow Colonel Webster to make that decision, and the job was hers. I was Cadet company commander (with the rank of private receiving two dollars and a half per month after deduction of the marital allotment). I became the second trainee with permission to live off campus. Reveille took place in pre-dawn darkness with many cadets still running as they answered roll call. About one morning each week, Al would cover for me by standing in front of the company for roll-call. Occasionally, I would appear at the last instant with a raincoat hiding my pajama top and jump off the bicycle while it was still rolling. It was embarrassing when both of us appeared in front of the company at the same time. This could have resulted in a court martial for Al, but I repaid him at exam time. He was convinced that the exam in engineering materials would be a quick ticket overseas. Between dates and studying for the calculus test which he knew he must pass, he had done absolutely nothing to prepare for this exam. We were in different sections of the course, so after taking the 10:00 exam for myself, I marched back into the same room, this time as Oscar Alton Carlson, Jr. There were a few puzzled looks from students, but I gambled on the fact that to an instructor, 100 young men in identical uniforms must look about the same. Al passed and we both escaped deportation.

As a member of the ASTP governing board, I enjoyed frequently seeing my name printed in the campus paper. There were few men left on campus, so we received abnormal attention. Our big projects were the variety show and military weekend. I was chairman of the military ball, so Peggy was the belle of the ball, and we enjoyed sharing the center of attention with Colonel Webster. The governor sent his "regrets."

Colonel Webster was an incredibly gentle and patient officer perfectly suited to grandfather our bright, fiendishly clever and rambunctious unit. One of the captains and one of the sergeants (both back from combat with the real army) thought our antics were anything but funny, but they gave up trying to get the CO to shoot a few of us as examples.

Earlier, I mentioned that Andy Rooney was in ASTP at another college, and I recall several classmates who were equally funny and

53

irreverent. This brings to mind Father Tom Phelan, who was Catholic Chaplain, then improbably became Dean of Humanities and Social

Al Carlson

Sciences while I was Vice President and Vice Provost at Rensselaer Polytechnic Institute. Father Tom was attending a national conference and when introduced to Andy, asked, "and what do you do?."

Andy explained that he was on television, and Tom confessed that he never watched TV.

"That's all right, Father - I don't go to church."

Years later, they were both at another meeting, and Andy approached Tom to say, "And I still don't go to church."

The incredible news of the atomic bombs at Hiroshima and Nagasaki burst on campus, and while jubilant, we were in a state of shock for a day or two. We finally realized that we would soon be disbanded and would join occupation forces, probably in Japan, to atone for our sheltered living of the previous year. Studying became even more difficult – few of us had any intention of practicing civil engineering, but we did recognize that credits earned now might shorten the completion of our degrees when we were finally discharged. Nevertheless, there was a general letdown among students and faculty alike, and a few deliberately hastened their departure, thinking that they might as well get overseas while some excitement remained.

We were a bit self-conscious in being asked to parade on V J Day. Army top brass feared that the only real military unit in that part of Oregon, Camp Adair, was too large and potentially explosive to turn loose on the little town of Corvallis, so we were obliged to perform. As cadet company commander, I had a prominent position in the parade, and Peggy came through with a snapshot from a cheap camera. There were a few commands of "PRESENT ARMS "but most of the crowd cheered our celebration without dwelling on the extent of our contribution to the victory.

ASTP in Oregon came to a quiet end just before Christmas of 1945. Peggy and I nailed up the big pine box containing the acquisitions of our brief married life, and flew home to Indiana to make the most of the few leave days granted en route to the infantry

Leading the Victors

replacement depot at Fort Ord, California. We had been busy enough to repress the reality of our inevitable separation until now, but we lived those few days as though they might be our last. The few hours were divided between our two families, 200 miles apart, with harmless family conversation during the day, and very limited privacy during the night.

The flight home used up the equivalent of two years of my take-home pay, so I set out for California alone in the cheapest possible day coach. Peggy loaded me down with food so that I need not fight the lines and the cost of a dining car. She need not have worried, because I was so sick that I ate practically nothing for three days. At night, I lay awake shaking with chills and listening to subdued giggles of the girls who worked the cross-country route the hard way – with strange servicemen in a railway coach.

Fort Ord looked better than expected. The winter sun was warm, and the fort was beautifully situated on the Pacific beach. We had entire evenings free from studying, sitting outside the serService club and listening to the surf while enjoying pitchers of beer. This was relaxation of a kind we could not remember. The ASTP veterans were scattered, but we were delighted to find many friends in the same or nearby units. No longer restricted to the rank of private, we sewed Private First Class stripes on our uniforms and many of us were promoted to corporal within a few days. Al's luck held, and he drew a private room with a staff sergeant who helped him garner the one open position as buck Sergeant. He loved pulling rank on us in his good natured way.

Barracks mythology held that "everybody" filched at least a field jacket, boots and sometimes even firearms by falling in with the rear rank of one of the units being outfitted for Japan. I suspected exaggeration in this tale, and certainly did not get my share of the loot, though I saw a few guys mailing parcels home.

After two weeks of inaction, we learned that our replacement battalion was being deactivated. I had really missed Peggy, so I immediately spent the pocketfull of quarters then required to call long distance and asked her to come to California. Without knowing whether she would arrive before or after we were shipped out, she jumped on a train and joined me in Pacific Grove, where I had rented a tiny apartment above a store. It was no place for a sweet and innocent young bride, but she used the daytime to explore a fairly good department store and a public beach within walking distance. By the time I was off duty and had fought my way through the long waiting line at the Fort Ord bus station, it was usually quite late. However, we would enjoy a small round steak and relax for a few hours before the early bus back to camp.

When the weekend finally came, we took an unforgettable bicycle ride around Seventeen Mile Drive on Monterey Peninsula, marveling at more mansions, Mercedes and Rolls Royces than we knew existed.

After a few more interminably long days and short nights, we finally learned our next destination – another reprieve and a return to Oregon with an engineering topographic battalion at Camp White, near Medford. The very last of our savings bought a Pullman ticket and the first week of rent for a furnished room operated by a nosy old witch who granted us the right to share a filthy kitchen with five or six other couples. We had no choice, and felt lucky that we could be together anywhere. Once again, Peggy came through in obtaining a civil service job, again in the headquarters of my unit. Our needs were few and our combined income paid the rent and permitted us to see some of the countryside near Medford.

After only six weeks, this unit also was deactivated, and we were transferred to Fort Lewis, Washington. I left at once with the advance party convoy, then took a short leave and looked for housing in crowded Tacoma. By reading the newspaper early, I was lucky enough to find a furnished room in a mansion overlooking Puget Sound. Peggy had remained behind to close out the records at Camp White and to pack our few belongings again. On the last evening, Al Carlson and Jack Thompson took Peggy out to dinner and then returned her to the room. Immediately, the landlady ripped her apart for not being able to remain faithful to me for even a week.

For the first time, I was able to take Peggy into rented quarters without being ashamed. We were among several civilized couples hosted rather than exploited by the delightful Russells. They had no children of their own, and enjoyed sharing their home with young service couples. This time, the kitchen was clean and the entire atmosphere was one of family rather than inmates. Light rain fell frequently when not continuously, a la Pacific Northwest, but we had occasional clear winter days when the view over the rushing tidal waters of Puget Sound was breathtaking. The estate across the street had extensive hillside flower gardens continuously renewed by a force of three gardeners.

In addition to this beautiful setting, our landlords provided a ride in their cabin cruiser, several trips in a remarkable Chevrolet with 400,000 miles on it, and a lead for Peggy to buy her first nylon stockings in several years. The only drawback was a four a.m. departure for Fort Lewis by share-the-ride in an old twelve-cylinder LaSalle. Peggy was able to wait until later for her ride to another civil service job. My evenings were short, yet I managed to finish a correspondence course in educational psychology at the University of California.

The overwhelming feature of the Tacoma area is Mount Rainier, rising 14,000 ft. right from sea level, which makes it an even larger bulk of mountain than Denali, whose summit is much higher. With good luck, we picked a beautiful weekend for the guided tour from Tacoma to Paradise Lodge. The day was so delightful that we rented skis and frolicked on twenty feet of snow. We bared every possible inch of skin and thoroughly enjoyed the day until a delayed reaction hit us. On arriving home, we noticed that the room was unusually dim. After a night of agony, we found ourselves nearly blind and covered with blisters the size of quarters which grew into half dollars and then dollars. When each blister finally popped, it was like spilling a glass of water in the bed. A week of rest, medication and reflection taught to us to respect the power of the sun at high altitudes. The top sergeant informed me that I could be court martialled, but the commanding officer was sympathetic and did not even count the lost time against my leave privileges.

With the coming of warm weather, we invited Al Carlson to spend an afternoon with us on Puget Sound. We had hoped to get the Russels' cabin cruiser, but this was already committed. It was a considerable step down to the rented rowboat and two horsepower motor. We chugged up The Narrows, lazed in the sun, enjoyed our picnic lunch, and started for home – and then we learned about tides. At the site of the infamous Narrows Bridge which shook itself to pieces in a steady though not strong wind a few years earlier, we realized that the motor was struggling to no avail – we were drifting farther from Tacoma all the time. In our frantic fooling with the engine, we managed to kill it, and we really became worried. We took turns rowing madly while the other two worked with the motor. Finally, it caught again, and thanks to our good physical condition and strong oars, we managed to inch toward home. Once out of the narrows, the motor took over nicely, and we collapsed for the remaining ride home.

The main conversation of servicemen in the spring of 1946 related to the famous point system for rotation and discharge. Our ASTP complex convinced us that we were marked men with a point total somewhere around minus 1000, and that we would be old men before we were freed. Nevertheless, in June we learned that our services were no longer required. We slipped through the discharge center as quietly as possible, fearing to the end that someone would recognize a mistake and cancel our orders on the spot. The dreaded never happened, and we were even given a little mustering out pay and a ruptured duck pin signifying honorable discharge. Most of the heroes had long since returned to their homes and were collecting their rocking chair money, so we were not particularly noticed.

CHAPTER SIX – LENGTHENING THE OREGON TRAIL

Peggy and I were both unemployed, so after a brief visit with my family in Boonville, we returned to Frankfort, where I helped with haying at the Irwin farm. Handling hay in the nearly opaque dust of a barn loft in sticky heat well over 100 degrees cannot be called enjoyable, but I felt considerable pride when a toothless laborer said to my father-in-law, "Hey, Ralph, that new hand you got is a pretty good worker."

No longer needed at the farm, I shamefully cashed a couple of 52-40 checks (veterans' readjustment pay), then "accepted" a position as deputy county surveyor. I was eminently qualified for the job through my training as a civil engineer and through my father-in-law's station as county commissioner. Post war inflation had not yet arrived, so the job paid five dollars per day plus all you could finagle. A fellow deputy was a private contractor, and after drawing up specifications for a construction job, he would accept the contract. It was wonderful that a person working for five dollars per day could afford an expensive car, airplane and speedboat.

Days were spent mainly in the field helping my boss run surveys for the large drainage ditches which are so important to the fertile but table-flat farms of central Indiana. I did accept one private commission to survey a drainage line for a new house in the woods (with some misgivings due to my lack of Engineering License and insurance). Two weeks later, my heart sank when my boss informed me that the ditch was finished and water had backed up into the basement of the fine new home. Then he quickly relieved me by reporting that the ditchdigger admitted he always worked by eye, paying no attention to the scribbles left by surveyors on their stakes.

My discomfort in taking jobs through family connections (Peggy also worked in the courthouse), and my observation of engineering-in-politics helped my decision that engineering was not for me. My original enrollment at Purdue, while probably life-saving, was really based on proximity, convenience and cost. My chosen major of public service engineering (invented by Purdue) no longer existed, and my completion of the civil engineering curriculum was decided for me by the army. I was ready to return to college.

We loved the mountains of Oregon and the year-round greenery of the Northwest so we decided to return to Oregon State College as the quickest route to a degree. My grades there were good, so I was admitted quickly. Getting there was something else. New cars were a bargain at list price, but involved under-the-counter premiums, so we saved and borrowed for a used car.

The Evansville newspaper listed a 1940 Chevrolet which we rushed to see. It seemed strange that it was not washed, but the owner was gracious enough to wipe off a bit of dirt to show that there was paint underneath – at least at that particular spot. The odometer showed 20,000 miles, which had to be the second time around, or perhaps the third, but we remembered how many miles Mr. Russell had driven his cream puff. I mistook the growl in the transmission for a purr of contentment, because the owner showed repair bills for recent transmission work. (Not enough work, because we soon replaced the whole thing). He graciously accepted $1,100, mostly Allen's, and we proudly drove off. The transmission made it as far as Frankfort. In December, we resigned our county positions, tied on top of the old Chevy a number of not quite bald tires which Peggy's father had hoarded during the war, recounted our cash total of $390 and headed west with an optimism not shared by our parents.

Well, not quite West. At that season, it seemed wise to avoid possible mountain blizzards, so we chose a southern route. Being South already, it seemed reasonable to detour through Texas and visit our best man, Al Carlson. At that point, we were fairly close to Mexico, so it seemed foolish not to go a bit farther and see a new country. Al agreed that he would like to join us in Mexico and share some of the expense, so that was quickly settled. Our parents threatened to let us rot in a Mexican jail, but they at least felt better that

Al would be with us. We committed to a route which would total almost 10,000 miles compared to the direct route of about 2300 from Indiana to Oregon.

The first few blowouts were almost a pleasure because we did not look quite as ridiculous and top-heavy. We would simply mount the spare and have another tire put on the rim at the next service station. Arriving at the Carlson ranch in Valley Mills, Texas, with most of our money, we enjoyed the December sun of Texas, then squeezed in Al and suitcase and headed for the border. Plotting our route was easy, because the Pan-American Highway was the only paved road to Mexico City. In the first few miles, we figured out the translation of the various road signs and the conversion of kilometers to observe speed limits. We were struck by the contrast of the modern highway and the primitive buildings which lined it except in the larger cities. Also, we noticed the pitiful sameness of the one-room esquelas – adobe walls, glassless windows, outdoor toilets and lack of any equipment excepting a very few textbooks.

Our combined budgets allowed $10 a day for food, lodging, gasoline, repairs and souvenirs, so we appreciated the abundance of dirt-cheap stubby bananas and free-flowing orange juice. After reflecting on the possible squeezing process, we switched to whole oranges which were even cheaper and which came in nature's own wrapper. Every travel book warned about dysentery, so we carefully avoided the vegetables and meats except to marvel at the fly covered carcasses hanging in stores. Only in Mexico City and Guadalajara did we venture into restaurants. The money exchange was so favorable that we could afford the finest for these limited splurges.

It was easy driving until we left the subtropical jungle for a maze of hairpin turns and passes approaching 10,000 feet in altitude. Cars with boiling radiators lined the road and I quickly learned to keep one eye on the temperature gauge while the other was fixed on the spectacular scenery. Between Peggy and Al, we had four eyes squarely on the highway, although they did suggest that perhaps one passenger should watch the landscape, another should watch the gauges, and the driver should watch the road. Only the numerous jeeps seemed able to navigate the steep grade without overheating. However, we learned how to minimize the problem by making the most of occasional downgrades to maintain momentum. Other American tourists seemed to have greater difficulty, because there was much evidence of blown tempers and blown radiators. At one emergency stop, we noticed that the cooling water had been carried up the mountainside several thousand feet. One section of highway was so torturous and fog ridden that 100 miles was considered to be an impossible drive for a day.

At meal time, we pulled off on a narrow shoulder, pumped up the old Coleman gas stove and heated a can of beans or whatever while listening to Al's portable radio. During one such meal, we saw a small group of Indians standing a short distance up the road. We were at the head of a steep trail, and determined through signs that they lived down this path. We had just begun to eat, and had no desire to pack up and move on, so we stepped aside from the head of the trail and motioned for them to proceed. They shook their heads and stood back – having no intention to pass that close to our stove and radio. The noise coming from the portable proved amusing, however, and they waited for several minutes before walking back up the highway. As we passed them later, we discovered that they were taking another trail which would involve a great distance of extra walking.

Not far into Mexico, the old Chevy developed a most annoying habit. Whenever we made a sharp turn to the left, the horn would blow and continue blowing until I fiddled with the wires in the steering column. Sharp turns were always in the small villages where a car was a wonder anyway, and it was most disconcerting to have crowds gather while I tried to silence the old monster. After several such occurrences, I finally ripped the horn wires loose. We soon learned that when you come around a sharp curve to find a flock of sheep or goats completely covering the road, it is better to have a horn. In Mexico City, we further learned that all traffic moves by the horns.

We settled ourselves in the big American motel and hired an English speaking taxi driver to show us the city. It would have cost five dollars per day plus scarce gasoline for a guide to drive our car, and for seven dollar a day we had a college educated driver risking his own fuel and fenders. The cathedral was awesome and we were fascinated by the old city built over a lake bed, but our greatest interest lay in the pyramids north of the metropolis. Hearts and lungs were tested by racing up the sides of Pyramide del Sol at 8,000 feet. Peggy found the descent a bit frightening, so Al and I each held one of her hands and we literally skipped down.

In the parking area, we met one of the racketeers who take over the parked cars. Each time one of us came within sight, he would move out of his semi-reclining position to furiously polish the same tiny patch of fender. After an hour of this game, we paid him what we thought it was worth, fully expecting him to be insulted by the Cinco piece worth about one cent. However, it probably only encouraged him, because it was a Cinco more than he had before.

Like all tourists, we had to haggle for a set of silver jewelry, spending fifteen minutes to arrive at the right price for a very heavy bracelet with earrings inlaid with polished black onyx. At an eighty percent discount, we were still not sure we had bargained long enough. Another local offered a figurine which had been long-buried, whether for millennia or days. The price started at several pesos and ended as an even swap for a tangerine.

After our various wartime accommodations, the height of luxury was a beautiful tiled motel in the mountains. For two dollars each, we had spacious rooms with access to a private chapel, armory and swimming pool. It made no difference to us that the pool was empty – this was the time before every little motel had its own pool, and we were really impressed.

The calendar said Winter, but it was a perfect climate. Days were long and clear, and snow covered mountains to the south and east of Mexico City were breathtaking. We desperately wanted to climb

Mount Orizaba, allegedly not very difficult despite its 18,000 feet, but time simply did not permit.

Teotihuacan

For our one big event, we chose a visit to the volcano of Paricutin. From its modest beginning just in front of a corn farmer about four years earlier, it had grown to a considerable size and its arms of lava had buried half a dozen villages. The eruption was at its most spectacular stage while we were in Mexico, so we felt this was the chance of a lifetime.

The road westward from Mexico City looked almost as good as the Pan Am highway, but we discovered one major difference – no gasoline. After passing several stations without fuel and noticing our gauge approaching empty, we stopped in a town to ask what we could do. A helpful young local directed us to a back alley establishment where we waited in line to buy very low grade tractor gas at triple the offical rate. We were in no position to bargain, so we filled the tank and calculated that with care, we might stretch it to Guadalajara, where the black market should not be so black. The cheap gas was no help in climbing mountains, knocking terribly at the slightest grade, but the engine kept running. It was exciting, being near the edge of civilization, and we drank in the "View of 1000 Peaks" and the serenity of Lake Patzcuaro with its colorful butterfly fish nets.

66

From there, we turned southward on a dead-end highway where we took lodging in a Moorish hotel and inquired about the volcano. We chose a night visit in the hope of seeing a display of natural fireworks, and it was pitch dark before we were anywhere near the jump-off village. That we ever found it was a marvel because of the twin barriers of language and total darkness. The road was neatly divided by a center line of boulders which was no problem until we came to a sudden hole on our side of the road. Swerving across the center line, we prayed fervently that the clash of stone against metal had not punctured our oil pan. Another swerve and crunch took place when we came to one of the unmarked bridges, consisting of two narrow planks, with the center stones continuing right up to the bridge. Obviously, the road was designed for vehicles with greater clearance than ours, but we trusted that the bridge timbers were set for the same wheel spread as the Chevy. After making it across the first planks, we relaxed just a bit.

When we finally reached the village, it was deathly quiet and without a sign of a light. In slamming our car doors, we roused a sleepy lad who told us that the guide had gone to bed for the night. Eventually, however, we had a guide and some swayback horses. The setting did not engender confidence, but having come this far, we could only trust that we were not in the hands of murdering thieves. We mounted the nags and started toward the volcano. Even without moonlight, the horses surely picked their way over the lava beds of dust and rock. When we were close enough to the molten lava that the trail was lighted, we saw that the horses were not equipped with any shoes for walking on the hot and jagged rock. The trail ended in a blind alley where the lava had divided so that it surrounded us on three sides. The intense heat forced us to shield our faces with our arms, but the Indian boy requested a large copper coin, and with a heavy stick, pushed it onto the lava. The stick immediately burst into flame and the coin folded to demonstrate how much heat remained in the lava several weeks out of the volcano.

From a more comfortable distance, we watched the fireworks with fascination. Out of the more distant fields of cooling lava rose lazy gases dimly lighted by a kind of phosphorescent glow. Newer lava beds were more active, with patterns of darkness and light continually changing as cracks appeared to reveal the red-orange interior. The crater rim was alternately hidden, then bathed in a red flare as it rumbled and worked up to a booming eruption. Fireballs shot 2000 to 3,000 feet above the rim, resembling a Roman candle. We knew from our reading that each ball of lava was the size of a five room bungalow. The red blobs rose and fell slowly until splashing on the slope to start the remaining slow but inexorable journey down the mountainside. The guide and horses stood patiently while we stared at the scene, our thoughts cycling through a wide range of impressions. We were wide-eyed and quiet, subdued in the knowledge that we were face to face with nature

Parcutin

in a way that we would never forget. Almost simultaneously, we three were aware of the lateness, of a chilling in spite of looking into the face of this natural furnace. As we turned away from the volcano, we saw our shadows as they might have been cast by neon signs flashing on and off in the streets of a city.

On the long ride back to the village, we could tell from the sounds of the horses hooves when we passed from a rock ridge into a stretch of soft volcanic ash. At these places, we pressed the horses into a fast trot, and they seemed to welcome the change of pace as much as we.

Fatigue had settled over us when we reached the village. Ours was the only automobile within miles, and we were relieved to find it intact. Our guide silently disappeared, leaving us wondering what had happened. A voice from the darkness said, "You pay me." We had no idea whether we should give money to this stranger so we asked what had happened to our guide. The voice answered, "He sleeber, you pay me." We finally decided that he must be the real guide and had sent us out with his son, so we paid him and left.

By the time we reached the hotel in Uruapan, it seemed obvious that not another person was awake within miles. In the morning, however, we found that our car had been stripped of everything removable. As we were working up to real lamentation, a little fellow appeared with his arms full of our missing accessories. He was guarding them so no one would steal them, and of course, he accepted a slight reward.

Time was running out, so we quickly drove to Guadalajara, where we were surprised to find a most modern city in the heart of the central plateau. By this time, we looked like genuine bums, yet were received warmly in a fine restaurant. Finding gasoline took some doing, but we started for the border with a full tank. We ran out of energy just before running out of fuel, so we slept in the car. With daylight, we located gasoline once again, and soon found ourselves back on the Pan American Highway with relatively frequent service stations. Presenting the Customs agents a bouquet of bananas and oranges, we recrossed the border without horn and without incident. To speed us on our way, Al took a bus from Laredo, and we headed directly for El Paso.

We saw Al once more, nearly thirty years later, while on a business trip for RPI. He was living near Dallas, selling real estate, and had named one of his sons Byron. This was a complete surprise, because he resisted both writing and phoning. We searched the net many times, but gave up. AFTER THIS BOOK WAS AT THE PRINTERS, WE WERE DELIGHTED TO REGAIN CONTACT THROUGH HIS SON, RONALD.

The map ahead looked pretty empty except for Great Bend National Park. We considered detouring to see it, but the region was barren and foreboding, so we skirted it and kept going to Carlsbad Caverns. We had earlier thrilled to the labyrinths of Mammoth Cave in Kentucky, but Carlsbad was especially impressive with its vast rooms and overpowering swarm of bats.

Now that we were truly entering the vast emptiness of the West, we were more than a bit apprehensive concerning the main bearings of the Chevrolet. For some time, they had been spraying a strip of oil on the highway at the rate of a quart per hundred miles, and the rate now was increasing. In the middle of desert country, one thinks about such problems, and during the middle of this very thought, we were startled to hear a horrible screeching and grinding. Convinced that our bones would bleach in the desert sun, we finally noticed that the noise ceased before the engine was turned off, and we concluded that we would gain nothing by sitting there. We edged cautiously forward and soon diagnosed the problem – not a faulty bearing, but a worn out speedometer cable which had allowed the rounded shoulders of the cable end to slip in the coupling. With great relief, we disconnected the cable and breezed on across the wasteland.

When we could drive no farther without sleep, we pulled off into the desert and folded ourselves as best we could on to the seats of the car. It was so cold that we frequently awoke with chills and would run the heater of the car for awhile before trying to sleep again. When daylight broke, we found that we were almost at the Painted Desert Inn. We stopped for breakfast, and masochistic curiosity confirmed that there had been vacancies at a reasonable rate.

On to the petrified forest, where we found a heavy chunk of colorful petrified wood to be carried around for ages before finding someone who could cut and polish it for bookends. Arizona also wowed us with the magnitude of Meteor Crater, the unexpected green forests and snow capped San Francisco peaks. Our time in Oregon had given us a deep fondness for both snowcapped mountains and Western

70

wild life, and we were seeing the best of both again after a separation of some months.

The lateness of the season gave us Grand Canyon practically to ourselves, which would not happen today. Hurried glimpses at each viewpoint were frustrating, but we drank in all the beauty which is possible in such a breakneck schedule and headed southward out of the park toward the stark beauty of Oak Creek Canyon.

Crossing the California desert from Needles to Los Angeles, we gorged on dried dates, stuffed dates, chocolate dates and many other flavors. We were finally relaxing in the certainty that our car worries were over, because we had heard glowing accounts of the used car market in Los Angeles. The old Chevy might bring enough to put us on easy street in Oregon. If these stories ever had been true, the situation certainly had changed. Several insulting offers convinced us that we should stick with the car all the way to Corvallis. Nevertheless, we pointed the Chevy in the wrong direction once again, and detoured to San Diego after a short stay in Beverly Hills with Len Herzog, who showed us the immensity of an empty Hollywood Bowl. While in A S T P, he had loaned his immaculate Model A Ford for a wonderful post-honeymoon circuit of Portland, Mount Hood and Crater Lake.

Our host in San Diego was pleasant enough, but we soon exhausted old times and discovered that we did not have much in common. We were now anxious to complete our journey, but could not imagine coming so close to Yosemite Park without a brief visit. Considerable snow had fallen in the high country, and the grove of sequoias was officially closed. This was no problem; scarcely a challenge until we lost one of our tire chains. There were some anxious moments driving through the snow until we reached the main highway, but we can never forget the unshared silence of the snowfall among the ageless trees. Our first view of Yosemite Valley was explosive. We emerged from a highway tunnel to see all at once the several waterfalls and the gigantic granite monoliths streaked with green forests, dusted with new snow, and capped by a brilliant blue sky. And not another tourist in sight.

71

Yosemite

Mount Lassen sounded like a pretty tame volcano after Paricutin, so we left it for a future trip. Mount Shasta dominated the trip in Northern California, always seeming to lie just beyond the next green ridge.

Peggy's Hoosier schoolmate, Marty, gave us overnight lodging in Klamath Falls, Oregon. As we left town, we reached the ice covered North slope of a hill at a curve where the highway was completely blocked by two log trucks. They were stopped so that the drivers could chat through their windows. Incredibly, this happened on the only major highway connecting California and Oregon. There was no stopping, so either reflex or luck caused me to head for the huge dual rubber tires of the truck. After the front end of the Chevy folded up against the comparatively soft target, we discovered that the tongue of the empty log trailer riding on the back of the truck had missed the windshield by six inches. Our brief stay in Klamath was renewed while the car was repaired and we cashed a savings bond to pay the deductible amount on collision insurance.

Despite our wandering and the accident, we arrived at Oregon State College in time to register for the winter quarter. Good fortune accomplished three basic and immediate goals – an apartment, a job for Peggy, and advertising the car for sale.

The ad produced immediate results in the breathless presence of three freshmen flush with money earned in the grain fields of eastern Oregon. I fully expected to be more forthcoming than the previous seller, but the demonstration ride spoke for itself. First, we had to push the car to make it start, then the brakes failed at the first intersection and we climbed a curb to avoid a collision. The horn was still inoperative, and at the end of the demonstration, I told them about the oil consumption and the accident. Expecting them to say something polite like needing to think about it, I prepared to say goodbye when two voices said at once,

"We'll take it."

This unbelievable deal made it possible to pay back Allen, stock the pantry and buy the bicycles which would be our slower, wetter but more dependable and affordable transportation until one was stolen. We found a well located apartment which made our first lodgings look even worse than they were, though the kitchenette was an extension of the living-room by about three feet. The carpet had a hole just the right size to practice putting, which I did frequently.

With Peggy's selfless, patient and essential contributions, married student life was a joy. In hindsight, we should have borrowed so that both of us could be in school, but student loans were not commonplace as they are now, and our depression upbringing made any form of debt a horrible prospect. The G.I. Bill, of course, was the farsighted congressional funding vehicle which really made it possible for so many of us to be in college. I was able to take courses that I really wanted and the pressure of A S T P was forgotten. My offhand taking of the Strong vocational interest battery showed that I had much in common with lawyers and school superintendents. In growing up as the son of a teacher, the superintendency seemed to be as exalted a position as one could want, so why not give it a try?

My serious homework was late at night, so Peggy would quickly squelch the alarm clock and tiptoe off to work in the morning. She sometimes returned to find me plotting golf with my veteran classmates/friends, but she rarely complained even though our other entertainment had to be low-cost or no cost. Midweek evenings sometimes included card games with neighbors, and on rare sunny weekends we rode bicycles around the countryside, occasionally splurging for a canoe rental on Mary's River. On one bright Saturday, we covered almost forty-five miles taking photos of the one-room schools remaining in Benton County for a term paper. More commonly, we rode in the ceaseless light rain – to class, to work, to market and to my student teaching (one of my Physics students was Sam Baker, later to break many records as a professional football star) – but only the front of our clothing was wet.

Willamette Valley rain might be harder to take since we have been spoiled by the sunshine state of Florida, but we usually took it in stride. The gentle patter was pleasant when going to sleep, though Peggy occasionally was homesick. Her quiet sobbing made me feel guilty and helpless, not knowing what to do except to hold her close to me. We were, indeed, a long way from home, but we loved the mountains of Oregon. The campus also had many landmarks of our courtship and marriage – the trysting tree, the quadrangle, and the fraternity house where Peggy lived when women dominated the enrollment.

Concern for Peggy made me hesitate when I was offered a slot as representative at the UNESCO conference in San Francisco. She urged me to take advantage of the honor even though we could not really afford the small share of expenses not covered by the college. The conference was inspiring and the byproducts were eye-opening. I refer not to our debate as to how nude girls got into the fishbowl at Nimbo's Bar, but to the revelation that a young professor in our delegation was a genuine Marxist. We were all a bit starry-eyed about ending all of the world's injustices, so a more subtle revolutionary might have planted some seeds in our minds. However, his sincere but warped mind could find nothing good in capitalism and nothing bad

74

in communism. San Francisco was a long car ride from Corvallis, and we had some heated debates, especially on the way home.

My bachelor's degree requirements were met quickly excepting one course, so my last months at OSC allowed me to complete most of a master's degree in counseling. I also studied and virtually digested the Oregon school directory. This little gem listed the educational qualifications and salaries of every teacher in Oregon. Its pages revealed career patterns which shaped my solution to the burning question facing many beginning teachers – big frog in a small pond, or small frog in a big pond? Portland's recruiter assumed that I would jump at his offer, especially since it guaranteed extra assignments to supplement the salary, and my professors suggested that I accept it.

All of twenty one years of age, and never over-blessed with humility, I saw no reason to begin at the bottom. Why not try to be a fairly big frog in a middling pond? I was not afraid of moving, and reasoned that a few smaller administrative assignments could bring me to a sinecure as principal or assistant superintendent where we could eventually have a comfortable income of perhaps $5,000.

Most openings appeared in late spring, and we daily haunted the lovably irascible placement director who thought of us as her boys. She was speechless at my gall in applying for administrative positions without a day of experience, but recognized an impressive dossier for my years. For two decades until her retirement, she supported me at every turn.

CHAPTER SEVEN – BIG FROG, LITTLE POND

Recruiters from the larger schools came to campus, but Peggy also typed several letters of application which resulted in an interview beyond bicycle range. A golf buddy, John Cannon, owned a war surplus Jeep which he was planning to drive to an interview on the near slope of the Cascade Mountains, so he offered to take me on across the mountains to Sisters, a village at the foot of the Three Sisters, each approaching 11,000 feet. Peggy and Aloha baked cookies and fried chicken (their respective specialties) and we took off in the very drafty and noisy little Jeep.

John's interview went well in the morning, then we continued through the Cascades, Hogg pass and on through corridors of huge Ponderosa pines into the little town of Sisters. Quickly reaching the far end of town on its single paved street, we turned around at the elementary building and the tiny brick high school and started looking for the chairman of the school board. He was working at his foreman's job at the local sawmill, and our interview was a standup affair competing with the scream of the huge circular saw. Assuming that I needed to measure up to the toughness of the town, I contrived to work a "damn "into the conversation. He must not think I was an immature kid! It quickly became clear that he was a former teacher and a real gentleman. In spite of myself, I impressed him, and a contract was mailed without my meeting the other two trustees or knowing much about the school district. The rest of my summer probably was more enjoyable because of my ignorance. They were hiring me on this theory: older men had done so poorly that they would try someone on the way up instead of the way down.

The previous superintendent had knocked out a teacher in front of a class of pupils to hasten his return to the calling of the Ministry. Many students and townspeople took a perverse pride in peddling the story that the school district was the worst in Oregon and would soon be padlocked. It was true that the State Education Department would have liked to transport at least the high school students to the neighboring town of Redmond.

My first contract was for $4,000, exactly the amount I had hoped for, and $1,000 more than I was offered to teach in Portland. But it was double the amount being earned by my father in Indiana after many years of teaching. My first offical duty was to hire two of my classmates to fill the completely vacant high school staff. In contrast, the larger elementary faculty was composed of local wives and was too stable for the good of the students. The elementary principal was a meek and threadbare little man who was reasonably competent and most cooperative.

The war had been ended long enough that my family was summoned to the Chevrolet dealer and informed that it was their turn to buy a a $1,000 car (plus $1,000 for largely useless accessories). Mother wrote that if Peggy and I wanted the car, they would deliver it to Oregon so that we might share with them a trip back to Indiana. Mother always was ready to travel. When they arrived with little brother Phil, we quickly showed off our region of Oregon, starting with the Pacific Coast and some deep sea fishing. It was one of those days when the ocean was beautiful, but with huge swells ripe for seasickness. Mother was soon at the rail, and when her false teeth went flying, she made a brilliant one-handed catch. This was the same mother who could catch a softball only by spreading her skirt or apron.

After loading our belongings on a car top carrier, we started our always circuitous but never duplicative journey to the east. In Sisters, we stopped just long enough to rent the only available house, then continued through the empty stretch of eastern Oregon, the bleak Craters of the Moon, an Idaho mud storm, the magnificent Grand Tetons, the scenic variety of Yellowstone, Devil's Tower and Mount Rushmore. To get across Lake Michigan, we had intended to take the ferry boat, but decided to drive all night instead of sitting in the car waiting for the dawn ferry. The trip was successful, though scarcely restful with five passengers and a huge amount of luggage/camping gear.

After a few days in the sweltering heat of Frankfort and Boonville, we were fully ready to return to Oregon, this time by way of Rocky

Sisters – First House

Mountain National Park and Salt Lake City.

The rental house was vacated the very hour we arrived in Sisters, and the outgoing tenants (a logger who was moving into my predecessor's house) insisted on helping us move our few belongings which were stored in the school. It was a hot Sunday afternoon, and midway through the job, he announced that we were going down to the tavern for a beer. My education courses had not discussed the merits of appearing in a tavern the very first Sunday in my new community, but intuition told me not to offend such a neighborly logger. Curious horsemen, mainly kids, had been raising clouds of dust on the street while we worked, so beer never tasted better, and if there was a WCTU in town, it was nowhere in sight.

The house was conveniently located right by the elementary school. It did lack a few conveniences such as indoor plumbing, central heating and furniture, but this was our first house and anything seemed fixable. We had a breathtaking view of the Cascades marred only by a neighboring backhouse in the foreground. At first, I used my forearm to frame the view more artistically, but I soon learned to do it with the mind alone. Our favorite view was at night when the

Sisters Vista

moonlight clearly pointed up the peaks which were ranged around us in a semicircle of nearly 100 miles.

Several curious boys gathered around to watch me unpack books at the high school, and one announced that they were going to give me

80

a hard time. Asked why, he told me that was the way it was done, and besides, the son of the fired administrator was their friend. All three new teachers were thoroughly tested, but not really given a bad time. We did not fit their experience with teachers who had served a series of short and miserable appointments at inferior schools. We were informal and flexible, so that the few barbs were merely deflected to the amusement of other students. Numbers were not a problem: during that first year there were about 200 elementary pupils, but only thirty-four in the high school.

The most troublesome were both boys of seventeen. Jimmy, who had quit high school, and Dewey who was on the verge of dropping out. Jimmy was a slim hipped young giant who could split a three-foot pine block with one blow of an ax. He hung around school a great deal, expecting to be ordered off the premises so that he could invite me to throw him off. Instead, I thanked him for showing up to help with the unpacking. Later, his older brother threw a roundhouse punch from a drunken haze and barely grazed my chin. De ja vu. As with the incident several years earlier, I was assured that I did the right thing in ignoring it, because he was frequently drunk and troublesome. He never caused the slightest trouble again.

Dewey fell in love with the brightest and prettiest girl in high school, so he could not drop out, and became my right hand and enforcer. My major objective of seeing Dewey graduate was finally realized, but it was not easy. From a previous pattern of using all of his energy and imagination to stay out of school, he now could not be kept out of the building, day or night. One of my first projects had been the addition of recreation equipment, and he became a ping pong addict, along with an immature custodian. Dewey's persistent presence was disturbing to the other teachers, and they questioned whether we were doing the right thing in keeping him in school. I had some doubts of my own until Halloween time. On this anniversary of what usually amounted to total destruction in the community, the student body marched up to our front door with Dewey in the lead and asked for the keys to my car. When I asked why they needed the car, he explained that they had been trying to push over our outhouse, and simply could not do it without the Chevy. Following a big laugh, they all trooped into our tiny living room, where Peggy made cocoa on the wood stove, and I showed the magical color slides taken on our various trips, We kept them all late enough that the damage to the town was noticeably lighter than usual, though other outhouses stood at the school entrances next morning. Without trying to determine who had done what to whom, I merely asked the boys if they would like to help return the articles to their owners. They pitched in willingly, and Halloween in that town has never been the same since.

My contract was a simple paragraph with the term of one year, although the job was complex. To the older citizens, I was "Professor." Professors simply did everything which needed to be done: superintendent, high school principal, part time math and science teacher, yearbook adviser, basketball and baseball coach when the part-time coach quit suddenly (my record of 4-16 made it easy for the new coach to gain acceptance when he appeared), substitute bus driver, and flagpole climber when the custodian proved to be afraid of heights. I was the community authority on certain matters of dispute or reference, guidance counselor and father confessor. As recreation director, I organized dances, mountain climbing and picnics. Most of the kids had never seen a city, so Peggy and I herded the entire student body and faculty on a bus which I drove on a 600 mile circuit of the state capital at Salem, Metropolitan Portland, the beautiful Columbia River Gorge, Mount Hood, and the Warm Springs Indian Reservation. We camped out in a city park and in an amusement park owned by the family of one of our teachers. The kids were as good as gold, mostly in gazing out of the bus windows at a whole new world.

I had a new vista, also. At Multnomah Falls, second highest in the U.S., we hiked to the top, and decided we should have a color slide from the top looking straight down. In order to get the camera beyond the protruding ledge, I had our clumsiest basketballer, Big Julius, hold my ankles. It is a spectacular picture which still causes Peggy to sputter.

Attendance improved, but deer season was approaching and our usually too mild-mannered lady teacher made the mistake of threatening failure to any truants. I needed to support her, but I remembered my own behavior as a student facing an identical ultimatum. My compromise pleased the community. Any tardy student would be excused if he had blood up to his elbows. In other words, a deer shot before school could be dressed without penalty – a purely pragmatic solution in a community depending heavily on venison for the winter meat supply.

If anyone today tried to duplicate the things we did, he would be condemned, sued, fired or shot, but it worked.

Peggy was soon visibly pregnant with Eric, but this did not stop her from splitting kindling when necessary to restart the fire in the pot belly living room stove or the kitchen range which provided our only hot water. Before long, we invested in an oil stove and a folding rubber bathtub. When the nights started getting below zero, we bought a chemical toilet.

Multnomah From Below

My blood even spilled briefly as a volunteer fireman. The town had a decent fire truck, but the hydrants were frozen and we had to resort to a bucket brigade. In fact, the whole town was frozen. The temperature hit forty below zero, and the wooden water mains were plugged with ice. Our house was without water for a full month, and this was near the climax of our first pregnancy. We kept the school in operation by carrying milk cans of water from a large spring, and chlorinating it in Lister bags for drinking.

At least, the big freeze could not hurt our outdoor plumbing. Water service was restored a slow foot at a time by groups of volunteers who alternated between pick, shovel and whiskey bottle. While trying to do my share, I was not very skillful with any of the three implements.

My hectic schedule kept me from being very supportive to the pregnancy. Lacking a telephone at the house, Peggy was to hang a white shirt out of the front door if she felt labor coming on. My students wondered why I kept looking out the classroom windows while teaching. It must have been reassuring when Mother Irwin arrived to help out, because Eric was almost due. There was no doctor in the community, although osteopathic physicians took up brief residence serially. One of them did an excellent job when I had smashed my eyeglasses all over my face in a darkened gymnasium.

The baby refused to come on schedule, so we relaxed as much as possible in entertaining Mother Irwin, who appreciated natural beauty more than anyone we have known. We took long hard drives, and were in the mountains nearly fifty miles from the nearest doctor when Eric was two weeks overdue. When labor began in earnest, however, we got to the Bend hospital in plenty of time for the March 17th delivery. The hospital was run by a Catholic order whose home was in Tipton, Indiana, so they fussed over her greatly, pretending to be terribly hurt when the name of Eric was chosen with complete disrespect for the day of Saint Patrick.

Sisters was small, but fertile, and we desperately needed more classrooms. By law, our bonding capacity was only $32,000 to cover land acquisition, construction, furnishing and fees for legal and architectural services. I found a young architect willing to gamble the preliminary planning, and he came up with a sufficiently cheap design connecting several Quonset Hut units. Restrooms had baffles instead of doors – a radical concept which had to be sold to the community. One key mother said, "I think it is a wonderful design for a primary school," and the subject was dropped.

Learning that the land adjoining the high school belonged to the Hill family, with headquarters in Minneapolis, I crafted a letter spelling out our financial plight and hoping for a favorable price. The eventual reply said they would donate the land, about 10 acres which later became prime highway frontage, for such a worthy cause. When I was singing the praises of this public spirited family at the next board meeting, an old timer snorted and "allowed as how" they could well afford to be so generous. He then related the tale concerning the alleged acquisition of the land by the Hills: Congress chartered a railroad to run from Bend to the Pacific, with a stipulation that alternate sections of public land on each side of the right-of-way would pass to the charter company when the first railroad car reached Hogg Pass at the summit of the Cascades. The old man swore that the only track laid was a short stretch near the summit. A box car was taken apart, hauled in by oxen and Chinese labor, reassembled and photographed. The company immediately proceeded to sell off the alternate sections, making millions over the decades, but still owned a few parcels including our new school ground. I never researched the accuracy of the story, but

Low Budget

the history of railroad building after the completion of the main East-West lines was replete with land grant scandal.

'We were now the proud owners of a field so covered with huge boulders that it was unuseable. With my usual brashness, I suggested to the PTA ladies that they might induce husbands to bring heavy equipment for a community work day. The idea caught fire, and with one week of organization, we assembled a fortune in heavy equipment plus a pickup load of dynamite. Never was such a good time had with such constructive results. The tavern owner brought a load of cold beer and the rock began to fly. I was more than a bit nervous at the juggernaut I had unleashed, but these men knew their equipment and they knew blasting. By Saturday night, the field was leveled and seeded, quickly becoming a primary school site and the high school athletic facility.

In that year of 1948- 49, I was not busy enough with starting a career and a family, so I became a citizen-soldier. John Cannon remained in the National Guard after more than his share of service with the Forty-first Division in the Pacific Theater of World War Two. He was now crossing the mountains to Bend each week for his required drill session. In visiting with the regular army officer who was advisor to the Oregon National Guard, he mentioned me as a good prospect for their officer ranks. In my two years of service, I was a trainee restricted to the lowest ranks, so I was flattered by the thought of being handed a direct commission. John assured me this would not take much time or responsibility, would complement my development as a school administrator, and should banish any guilt feelings for my good break in A S T P. Further, I would enjoy new friendships. John recognized that being a chief school officer was inevitably a rather lonely assignment.

John was correct on all counts – for a few months – until I was suddenly drafted as company commander of the unit. I was still a very young and green second lieutenant in a position normally held by an experienced captain. My responsibility for the 100 plus men did not worry me as much as the huge inventory of weapons and other equipment for which I signed my life away (the supply sergeant assured me, as he did my successor, that it was all present even though there probably had been gaps for many years). Next, I learned that I was also ex-officio a member of the Armory Board. This required a minimum of a second long evening each week round tripping more than forty miles to Bend. It also required my involvement in such national defense priorities as renting the armory to promoters of professional wrestling and preventing the little old lady fans from throwing folding chairs into the ring. In addition to losing time and sleep, I was spending considerable money. I R S added insult to injury by forcing me to pay income tax on my token pay even though it did not cover the commuting cost. This interpretation was later changed in favor of common sense, but not in time to help me.

Drill sessions were serious business, with too little time to convert our rag tag contingent into an effective military unit. In theory, this final miracle was accomplished during two weeks of active service each summer at Fort Lewis, Washington. Rounding up the last reluctant privates to leave town was quite an experience. We deputized a few squads of the more reliable members to search out the unwilling in various bars and beds, and drag them to the train. Once in camp, we lived in tents which were not easily secured, so I spent some of my time bailing men out of jail. I was even less prepared for the charge by a private that he was solicited by one of our better officers, a First Lieutenant whose bars were actually senior to my brand new ones. While he meekly denied the charge, he preferred resignation to facing his accuser.

Many times have I praised the Lord that I was not required to lead my infantry company into a crisis like Korea, Vietnam or Iraq. Still, I enjoyed the physical conditioning and leadership challenges – even briefly considering an Army career. This was prompted by my admiration for Colonel Alfred, who later served and suffered in Korea. This same outstanding officer and gentleman counseled me out of the plan, saying that the public schools needed leadership even more. His glowing service reports made me hope and trust that his counseling was not calculated merely to protect the army from me.

Fort Benning Jump School

To accelerate my seasoning as an officer (and to afford a trip to Indiana with our new baby), I volunteered for parachute training at Fort Benning, Georgia. The major who chaired the Armory Board was in the car business, so we traded the 1948 Chevy for a 1949 Dodge which we picked up at the factory. Until later in the summer when Peggy joined me, I lived in the bachelor officer quarters at Fort Benning with a group just graduated from West Point. They happened to be Mormons from Utah, and I have never known finer young men. They were in perfect physical condition, so I was at first apprehensive about keeping up with them in the summer sun of Georgia. In fact, I was much better off than several regular army officers who suffered greatly in terms of physical pain and professional pride. Officers and enlisted men were totally integrated except for housing, and most of us eventually found that we could do endless situps, twenty-five or thirty pushups, and miles of running in full uniform and boots.

Our drill sergeant was perhaps the finest teacher I have known at any level, handling both privates and field officers with toughness and consideration. His leadership on the five mile runs made it impossible for us to complain or feel abused. While we were struggling to run forwards, he would run backwards alongside the company, singing out cadence with a repertoire of clever ditties. He even cleaned up the lyrics in deference to the transparently innocent and sincere young Mormons. When a trainee messed up, the sergeant joined the guilty one in the customary 10 pushups at roadside, then sprinted to catch up with the rest of us. My admiration caused me to urge him to teach in high school, but he loved his life as a paratrooper.

Along with physical toughening, we took glider training, then started jumping from a succession of platforms with increasingly diabolical harnesses. After the bone rattling experience of the thirty-four foot tower, jumping with the cable fixed to your chute, it was a pleasure to graduate to the 250 foot towers where we jumped with a parachute guided in a fixed track, then with free chutes.

For several weeks, we barely had strength to crawl back to the barracks and flop for the night. Eventually, however, we reached the point where we wanted to get off the base for a change. We had been warned about the dangers of Phenix City, Alabama, which most trainees sample and many regret, so a couple of us settled for the bistro nearest the main gate. It looked quite refined, but upon conversing with the young lady in charge of social arrangements, we realized that we were not exactly in Sunday school. We were buying only beer, but this Helen of Joy seemed anxious to talk about her career managing several cotes of doves between Fort Benning and Montreal. She was aware of the Mann Act and its penalties, but accepted the risk to better serve her country and its soldiers. It paid better than other jobs even for a girl with good looks, but for a slightly crosseyed plain Jane like herself, she claimed it was sheer pleasure. Business was booming, but she did not look to be as happy as she pretended.

As paratroop training drew to a climax, we took the crucial physical test and began to pack the parachutes we would use in our five required jumps from the C-119 flying boxcar. I found a room near the fort, met Peggy in Atlanta, saw the great Civil War cyclorama, and spent a pleasant weekend at Okefenokee Swamp and St. Augustine. Peggy was at the exhibition field when we made our first jump, and had no way of knowing that my parachute was one of the 99% which opened correctly. She saw one jumper come down hard, though safely, entangled in another man's parachute. The first man in my stick froze long enough at the door that while I landed in the middle of the plowed field, the colonel bringing up the rear found himself dangling from a pine tree. The first jump was exciting, but not difficult for me – perhaps because of my flying.

It was pure terror for some, and my experience did not get easier as the series progressed. On the third jump, I was oscillating severely, and hit the ground on the downward swing of the pendulum, landing on my back, to which was strapped an M1 rifle. (Should I wonder why I have some back problems?) The final jumps were routine, and I mentioned earning some easy money by jumping into shopping malls. Peggy quickly killed that idea.

My jump wings were awarded just in time to hurry back to Indiana and retrieve Eric. We met some Oregon friends who decided to share the cost of the drive back with us. This time, we detoured far enough to see the fabulous Glacier National Park.

Our second year in Sisters was more routine than the first. The new high-school teachers were short on experience, but long on determination, and discipline was not as much of an issue. Bill Edwards was a little dynamo, creative in the classroom and eager to take on every possible coaching assignment. He and Jeannie also had a baby boy, so our families had much in common and got along beautifully – even when we found ourselves snowbound at their house after an evening of cards. We lived only blocks apart, but the snow had fallen to a depth of three feet.

Though strictly a snowplow skier, I introduced Bill to the sport, and he became both addicted and expert. In turn, he taught me fly-fishing to catch the wily trout. I had not appreciated how totally absorbing the sport can be so that job and personal problems automatically are forgotten. We hunted deer, with absolutely no damage to the species, and climbed the lesser mountains, once taking the entire student body. Upon starting down, someone decided to make a race of it, and we were suddenly scattered all over the mountainside. Once again, we returned with no broken bones or missing persons.

Bill and I frequently planned to climb the Three Sisters, but never made it. He later took a position in Europe, and climbed all of the Alps. On one occasion, we hiked about twelve miles into a primitive area to sample some of the rarely fished lakes, and we took our new hunting rifles in case we tangled with a bear. It was a beautiful late summer day, so we spread out our sleeping bags under a dense evergreen and proceeded down into a crater strewn with boulders the size of ten foot dice. A cloudburst came from nowhere, so we and our spread out gear were totally soaked before we could make our way out of the crater. We attempted to burrow into heavier undergrowth and to build a fire to dry out, but the driving rain penetrated everything. It was growing quite dark, and it now appeared the deluge would continue all night. Not wanting to freeze in position, we decided to hike out to civilization. Shouldering our gear with its additional weight of water, we bent our heads to the storm and started the long hike out. We turned the flashlight on occasionally to see that we were still on the trail, but we really knew that from the rush of water around our ankles. Finally, we found a lean-to where we could build a fire with the matches Bill kept in his underarm pocket. The fire restored circulation in our fingers and toes, but was of little comfort when we climbed into our sleeping bags. After squirming miserably for awhile, we decided that the brain numbing automation of the trail was a lesser evil than the frustration of a wet sleeping bag, The night seemed endless, but we stumbled out of the woods at the trail head just as the storm was letting up and darkness was giving way to pre-dawn.

Bill's enthusiasm helped to sustain my own, and together, we initiated many fine projects. When he stayed on as administrator after me, he built the school into one of the best of its kind.

Among the town characters were the barber who cut hair only on those few days when there was no season for either hunting or fishing, and whose sporting activities were supported by his teaching wife; the highly educated forester who combined with his wife to destroy their

91

furnishings from time to time; the big Swedish janitress who called me out of bed regularly to confess that she still could not figure out how to push the reset button on the furnace; and George Wakefield, the garage owner. This was no ordinary garage. He operated several lumber trucks, sold appliances, tinkered with Rube Goldberg gadgets and generally enjoyed life. When he was too busy to grease my car, I would run it up on the hoist and do it myself.

The mill owner, a Christian gentleman who adopted a large family, built a private airport, so George bought an airplane as a toy. When I mentioned my bit of flying, he took me on an unforgettable flight down the spine of the Cascade Mountains. The formations of drifted snow, in areas never traversed during winter, were fascinating. As we flew over the mountain peaks, we could see bits of snow slough off the high slope, picking up material and momentum until they became huge snowballs, then avalanches. From a distance, the avalanches are soundless and are slow motion action, but if you hike to the base of the peaks in summer and wait quietly, you will hear periodic rumbling almost like thunder.

Cascades From The Air

George and I were both preoccupied with the scenery, and thoughtlessly flew on the east side of Mount Jefferson, second highest in Oregon. The air mass almost always moves from the West, boiling upward and then downward in a tremendous downdraft. The plane lost

92

2,000 feet of altitude in seconds, while the camera strapped around George's neck was battering his chin. The little airplane kept its wings and avoided spinning out of control, so it was merely one more exciting lesson for both of us.

My top priority for the school was to impact the pattern of near total attrition before graduation. One strategy almost unheard of in rural communities was sex education before the age of pregnancy. I knew that it could be an explosive issue, so I carefully primed the board, borrowed a fairly conservative film produced by the Brown trust, and appealed to the local theater owner to host a morning preview, complete with coffee, for eighty-six curious mothers and one skeptical father. Following the showing, parents with children above the threshold age were asked to indicate in writing whether they wanted their children to see the film. Support was unanimous with only the expressed disappointment that younger siblings could not also see it. In the years following, there were indeed fewer pregnancies and dropouts.

It developed that the head custodian had been getting his own sex education through a peephole between the boiler room and a girls' locker room. Interestingly, he had served on the school board for forty years, was chairman when both buildings were constructed, and personally shaped the floor plan. Despite his political power in the community, he quietly turned over his huge key ring when I revealed the bomb shell – his own granddaughter was the one who told me.

Another retention strategy, unknown except in the most progressive high schools, was our little work-study program which granted fractional credit while some of the seniors served internships in local businesses. A State Education Department examiner grudgingly admitted that our programs were working, but said, "I hope you realize that you are making the same salary as our boss." Rex Putnam had been Superintendent of Public Instruction forever. I acknowledged that I had been treated very well and would try to give the community full value.

I decided not to show the examiner our bomb making unit. The one boy who clearly should attend college was obsessed with explosives, and I decided it would be better to channel the interest than to ignore it. We made a simple explosive, then took a select group deep into the woods where we blew several rotten stumps into smithereens. That appeared to satisfy the boys' curiosity, but can you imagine a teacher doing such a unit today?

En route to a basketball game, we crossed Crooked River Canyon, which the kids explained to me was so deep that a dropped match would pick up sufficient speed to ignite by air friction. I explained that this could not possibly happen and demonstrated with a wooden match. Swirling air currents carried the match against the canyon wall, starting a good brush fire 300 feet below us, and convincing the kids that air friction was not a myth.

At age twenty-two, I must have looked awfully young to be a school administrator. However, the community was not only tolerant, but grateful, and helped me laugh at my embarrassments. On another field trip, I gave much fatherly advice to the beginning skiers, barely younger than I, and guess who was the only person to be carried out of Hoodoo Ski Bowl on a toboggan?

Sisters has become a very popular tourist/condo/dude ranch destination. Some of the sage brush and lava then available for one dollar per acre now is irrigated from the Deschutes River and is worth thousands.

CHAPTER EIGHT –
BACK TO SCHOOL; DELIVERANCE AGAIN

I had written most of a master's thesis, but the data were now stale, so I was anxious to get back to graduate school. The board had given a generous raise of $1,000 after the first year, already meeting the long

View from Rescue Sled

range goal of $5000 plucked from the school directory. My father, among others, wondered whether I was in my right mind to leave such a job and go back to school with a young family. However, I had not used quite all of my GI Bill credits in completing my private pilot license, and Peggy was willing to work again.

There was no question that I would earn a doctorate, but I was incredibly naive as to how the system worked. Rupert could have explained it very easily, but long distance telephone was very expensive at that time, and we rarely called anyone. I simply assumed that in the highly centralized Oregon state system of higher education, my good graduate record at Oregon State College would admit me to the University of Oregon Graduate School. Success there surely would be rewarded eventually by a fellowship. It was not automatic, but my simplistic reasoning did work out.

We took a rented truck across MacKenzie Pass to a furnished room near the University of Oregon, because Peggy was going to spend the summer visiting in Indiana while I went to summer school for a head start. Late in enrolling because of National Guard active duty, I talked hard and fast to gain permission to take 10 credits during the time remaining. To make matters more interesting, Peggy was scarcely settled in Indiana before the Korean war heated up. A lottery was taking place to determine which National Guard divisions would be called. Fearing that my military luck might run out, especially with fresh paratrooper wings, we panicked into having Peggy fly back from Indiana without Eric. Then I proceeded to shorten my summer course even more by rushing through some all night term papers and getting permission for early exams. Having earned 10 credits in two and one-half weeks, we proceeded on a leisurely trip back for Eric. This time, we detoured to include Victoria, B.C., Banff and Lake Louise. This was completely contrary to my normal role as a skinflint, but we never regretted the madness.

Once again, we started back to school with practically no savings. Just before we left for Indiana, Dr. Babcock (later President of the American Society for Curriculum Development) asked me how I was financing my graduate education. I told him that for starters, we would sell our almost new Dodge. He had been impressed by my creative flurry of credits, so he asked Dean Paul Jacobson whether anything could be done to help me. In his dry manner, the Dean advised me that applications had been processed some four months ago, but he not only arranged a teaching assistantship under the irascible Dr. Huffaker, but also recommended me for the part time position of Executive Secretary of the infant Oregon School Boards Association. The hourly pay was fair at $2.50, but since I was manager of the limited budget, I could not bill all of the hours actually worked.

In addition to writing and printing the association newsletter, I lobbied the legislature for an enabling act allowing school boards to pay association dues from public funds instead of their own pockets (most states already allowed this). The lobbying project allowed me to meet Mark Hatfield, then a political boy wonder who had been Dean of students at Willamette University and President of the Oregon Senate in his twenties. He later became a liberal Republican U.S. senator and a continuing idol, though I was saddened when he eventually paid the inflating costs of campaigning by accepting funds from special interests like all the other politicians.

My lobbying proved successful, and the position allowed me to collect material for a master's thesis on the attitudes of school trustees. I had received permission to go directly from the bachelor's degree to the doctor's, but remembering that I had a growing family to support, I switched plans to finish a master's.

Accepted into the low rent ex-barracks housing, we graduated to the ground floor

Big Boots

where we patched and painted enough to make it livable. We were blessed with lovely neighbors – Norma and Bill Evans – who shared our interest in education and became quite fond of babysitting Eric. Norma's experience as a nurse was most helpful, and they seemed delighted to have a baby next door. Eric was at a lovable age –

97

stumbling around in my army boots and helmet. Second son Philip was on the way, so we got permission to put an electric clothes dryer on the back porch to help launder the cloth diapers which were still the norm.

Starting the year with a nearly new car and one child, we soon traded for a very old car and a second child. The new baby brought complications for Peggy, both physical and because of the necessity to quit her job. We soon discovered that we had traded down a bit too far, to a 1941 Plymouth. Not only was the engine intermittent, but at every lurch, the water which mysteriously accumulated inside the roof would discharge itself down my trouser legs. Finally, on a lobbying trip to Salem, the car died so decidedly that I traded on the spot for a 1946 Ford. This lasted us through the year – barely – until Providence directed to Peggy a small inheritance which covered a new car. This came from cousin Jeanette "Nettie" Dunlap, and Jeanette was Peggy's middle name.

In working for Professor Huffaker, I turned out thousands of statistical computations for his various field studies. He was not talkative, and I usually figured out what he was doing the hard way. However he liked my study on the attitudes of school trustees, and we developed a mutual respect which led him to refer to me as "my boy." What really impressed him was my handling of a final exam to prove without question the collaboration of several football players. We both liked athletics, but were not about to waive the minimal requirements for athletes to earn credit.

My final decision to go back to work was late in the season, so job searching was somewhat haphazard. I traveled to Roseburg to discuss an assistant principalship which I did not want, but while there, I heard of a chief school officer opening up the North Umpqua River at Glide. On a very long chance, I called board President Bob Franks at dinner time, learning that he was just leaving for a board meeting and would interview me even though the board had never seen my placement credentials. We drove out into the early evening smoke of a forest fire which appeared to be just over the ridge. Eventually, all board

98

Glide High School

members arrived and started discussing the position with me since I was the only visitor and the newspaper reporter either had forgotten the meeting, or had not been notified.

The board members were as conservative as the ancient building in which we met, but recognizing the need to upgrade and update, they had already broken ground for a fine new high school.

I later learned that the vacancy came quickly when the superintendent physically tangled with a board member whose wife was a teacher. The board had finally agreed on a replacement, but he accepted another lower risk position, and it was now summer time. Unbelievably, without seeing any credentials or recommendations, the board all agreed to take a chance on me if I would accept the same salary I received in the smaller district of Sisters. They also offered a house on the school grounds at a nominal rent. These were not the most flattering terms for a person with a shiny new master's degree, but it was late for me as well as for them, and I could see much promise in the district. It had recently consolidated an area of 1200 square miles, and the California-Oregon Power Co., or COPCO, was spending $100 million on a series of dams and power houses. I was moving from the poorest second class district in Oregon to the wealthiest first class district (tax base, certainly not wealth of residents).

Toketee Falls

The district had three distinct constituent groups: native ranchers, relatively transient loggers and power company employees, only a few of whom would remain after the projects were completed. The ranchers were the dominant group, but I was delighted with one board member with a wise head and a strong voice when needed who taught school before becoming a highly successful lumberman.

Quickly accepting the terms, I arranged for the board to receive a copy of my papers so they could substantiate their excellent snap judgment. Peggy and I started planning the move. I was still in the National Guard, reporting to battalion headquarters in Salem, though they had allowed me to attend drills near the University in Eugene. Korea was still hanging over our heads. When I asked the colonel what to do about drill attendance now that I was 100 miles farther from headquarters, he suggested a letter pleading incompatible occupation. He strongly endorsed my request, and I was flabbergasted to receive a letter from the general allowing me to resign. WHAT A RELIEF!

Now I could play catch-up on my new job. There were still vacancies to be filled at the remote little school far up river where no

100

one wanted to go. Learning about a couple from Salt Lake City who were interested in the openings, I arranged to take them to the remote school in our old Ford, and for the man to drive back the school bus which needed considerable repair before school could begin. Now a scenic paved highway, the Toketee Road in 1952 was a single lane carved out of the rocky bluff. At many places, a passenger needed to get out and guide the driver over sharp boulders which could easily puncture the oil pan. Normally, it took more than three hours to travel fifty miles. Before ever reaching their intended home, the couple decided not to leave the relative civilization of Utah for this desolate gorge, but the man kept his promise to drive the school bus back down the canyon.

Near Miss

Rocky Road

One small problem – it was now dark, and the Ford generator died, allowing the engine to function but without lights or horn. We agreed that the bus would drive even more slowly than usual, and I would follow the tail lights. The first few miles were fine until we hit a stretch of fairly decent road where the bus literally left me sitting in a cloud of dust. Eventually, the bus driver realized that he was not being followed, so he turned around at the first opportunity and came back. At the second parting, we were

101

on the edge of a high cliff above the river. As the black gulf between the Ford and the bus increased, so did my sweating, so I stopped again. A shower of sparks told me that the bus driver was staying as far from the river as possible.

This time, he was gone for almost two hours. When he finally appeared, he asked why I did not signal him with lights or horn if he was getting away from me. What lights? What horn? By now, it was early morning, and Peggy was terrified. I had left her with two baby boys in a house without furnishings or electricity. She finally woke up some elderly neighbors, and the police were just beginning a serious search when we rattled in.

The aborted staff for Toketee Falls headed back to Utah, but I had appealed for help to brother Rupert, a professor of education at the University of Illinois. He asked his classes if they knew of married elementary teachers who would like to live in the Cascade Mountains and save a lot of money. We paid well, offered supplementary employment and free housing, and there was nowhere to spend money. Rupert had a couple who jumped at the bait, so he committed the positions without knowing of the Utah couple. As it turned out, I was fortunate in several respects that they turned tail for Utah.

Ray and Dorothy Coffenberry appeared with daughter, Sarah, and they did a wonderful job for several years until he called in the middle of the night asking for help. The hydroelectric project had no telephones excepting their own primitive service which piggybacked on the power lines with a great deal of static. When I needed to call that school, I would dial up the COPCO office near Roseburg. An employee would internally call Toketee headquarters, then hold the Bell System receiver back to back with their internal receiver while Ray and I shouted our communications, sometimes for an hour. Fortunately, someone was on duty twenty-four hours.

Dorothy had suffered a nervous breakdown, probably from the combined effects of an unexpected second child and worry about fire safety in their apartment above the school. The nearest psychiatric hospital was in Portland, nearly 300 miles distant, so we told Ray to

102

leave the children with us during the seven weeks of treatment for Dorothy. Sarah was not much older than Eric, and it worked out well. We were shocked when Dorothy returned with white hair, and she was clearly a different person. They stayed at Toketee for years until Ray accepted a position at Myrtle Creek, which named a building for him.

About one month before the opening of our second year at Glide, I learned that one hundred families were being moved to a new dam site forty miles on beyond Toketee, which we had assumed to be the end of the earth. The COPCO Superintendent (who delivered about ninety percent of the total taxes to our district) asked what I was going to do about education for the children of an extremely fertile crew. My reply was, "I can't do much, but working with you, we will provide good education." He came up with a solid surplus building in another camp, sliced it into sections and reassembled it after a move of one hundred miles. The community at Toketee helped us charter an instant PTA at Lemolo Falls, and the wives invited their husbands of the new trailer community to an old fashioned school raising. With a budget of $1,000 for paint, curtain material and light fixtures, we had a decent one-room school within the month (operating two shifts because even more employees with children volunteered for the project). Better yet, we had the strongest parent-teacher association in Oregon. One teacher was found in the project, and Rupert came through again with promises of gold in the mountains.

Another digression: George Churchill, the head forest ranger for the District took me on a five day pack trip to visit his fire lookouts. Our dependable old pack horses picked their way up cascading creek beds and lava rock stairways where we thought no human had walked. Suddenly, we came upon several lengths of huge and heavy cast iron pipe lying in virgin forest. George explained that during the Gold Rush, Chinese laborers had carried such pipe deep into the Cascades for a brief attempt at hydraulic mining.

The construction workers generally had young families, but there were a few reaching high school age, both at Toketee and at Lemolo.

We found families in Glide to house them, and weather permitting, we took them home on the weekends.

Most superintendents of other school districts envied our tax base windfall in good humor, but the Oakland district decided they would share our wealth. They filed suit in the District Court requesting an outrageous gerrymander snaking through a region of mountains and no roads to one of the hydro projects. Working with a young attorney in Roseburg, I developed maps, charts and a debate-inspired presentation which ended the case in one session.

Phil Hiking

We were a long way from our Hoosier families, so on three occasions, I volunteered for a free trip while saving district funds by delivering school buses from the factories in Indiana and Ohio. In one case, I was able to recruit a teacher by offering to move his family furnishings free of charge. Otherwise, the cost of moving that distance by Railway Express frequently was greater than the value of the goods. The board went along with my desire to seek different scenery each trip, so we were able to visit virtually every national park in the West. On one trip, we included Peggy's mother, who loved travel just as much as my mother, and by stacking a few of the bus seats, we made room for an old mattress which became a large playpen for our baby boys.

The board had a good laugh when another superintendent made headlines for taking similar delivery of a bus – his board felt that bus driving was undignified for a superintendent. His obvious mistake was in making the trip without prior and unanimous board approval.

While not hung up on dignity, co-pilot Peggy and I found the driving challenging. This was before the Eisenhower interstate highways, and although roads in the West were good excepting the endless mountain switchbacks, parts of the Midwest were tricky. U.S. twenty was the most direct route through the corn country, and stretches of this older artery were so narrow that the rear dual wheels actually hung off the edge of the pavement. When going through towns, it was not uncommon to have ninety degree turns where the big bus needed to swing into the oncoming lane of traffic. After a while, Peggy learned that if we were approaching a town on her driving shift, I could slide into the driver's seat from the left as she was sliding out, and there was no need to find a shoulder wide enough to pull off and change drivers. Our worst experience was on a Sunday in St. Joseph, Missouri. It was 117 degrees when the battery failed and I started walking to find an open garage with a large enough battery. The city was big enough to produce one, but this was before credit cards, and the owner was not about to accept a check from Oregon. When we finally reached Oregon by pooling funds with Peggy's mother, we had a nearly empty gas tank and ten cents in cash.

Before one trip, I learned that the county unit of the National Education Association was looking for a delegate to represent them at the convention in New York City. There would have been dozens of volunteers, but the budget allocation of forty dollars would not go very far. I was delighted to learn that Dad was a delegate from Indiana, so we drove together and shared a room. Our big night out was to see Kismet on Broadway. Again, much of the thrill was missing because Peggy was back in Indiana. Still, it was the only time I could recall being alone with my father.

For the new high school, I hired a principal who was very bright and energetic but who managed to alienate the community. He could communicate with me, and I with the locals (well enough that when our school budget passed by a vote of 175 to 1, it really bothered me that I had failed to convert someone). What I overlooked was the fact that culturally, I was at the edge, and the principal was beyond me. He had attended an Eastern prep school, and was convinced that soccer was a much better game than football for high school. I had listened, and had no problem with trying to introduce the sport, presumably as a club activity.

Just after I walked into a board meeting one night, the President told me it had already been decided that the principal had to go. Instead of adding soccer as an activity, it was claimed that he ordered the athletic department to substitute it for six-man football, of which we were the state champions. I protested that he held a valid contract, which the board honored in the form of a well paid teaching position. They had supported me in every other situation, but on this one, they would not bend. Having reached this stage, the problem had no good solution. My failure was in not seeing the problem coming.

The principal elected to serve the year as a junior high teacher just around the corner from my office. He was very professional in his teaching, but extremely bitter, and it was a long year. It was difficult also for Peggy, who had been very close to his wife and children, about the same ages as ours. The families wanted to remain in touch, but he would have none of it. Years later, he asked the regional accrediting association to investigate whether there was anything illegal or improper in the incident. I gave them the records, and they found no cause for action.

Faced with the administrative vacancy late in the season, I remembered that Ray Talbert, who had been my ally in the debates with the only genuinely Marxist professor I ever knew (contrary to the claims of Senator McCarthy who was positive that they dominated faculty ranks), had made a solid reputation as teacher and assistant principal near Portland. He jumped at our principalship and performed extremely well for years.

I had matured somewhat since Sisters, but still made decisions outside of the textbook solutions. The new building budget expired before we could landscape the grounds, which were ten per cent soil and ninety per cent rocks. I decided to offer our discipline cases a choice between the usual detention and half that much time spent in constructive labor, carefully avoiding dangerous situations. A few eyebrows were raised, but we were careful to avoid coercion, and the volunteer miscreants developed considerable pride in the lawns as they appeared.

Our athletic department included some talented and pleasant coaches, but there must have been something other than Gator Ade in the cooler. The six-man football coach was a fine motivator, and delivered our first state championship. However, he over-motivated a fourteen-year-old student, fell madly in love with her, and quickly married her despite the fact that his application for employment had referred to a wife and child in Nebraska who would be joining him. In the very late summer, I received a call from the county school superintendent in Sun Valley, Idaho. Our ex-coach was applying for a principalship, so I told the whole story. The caller thanked me, but said that he probably would hire the man anyway, because the other finalist was a religious fanatic. Later, I learned the rascal told his superintendent that his wife of fourteen had two years of college, so she was hired as a music teacher.

Next, the head basketball coach, who had a lovely wife and two darling daughters, went ape for the girls physical education teacher who was the least likely temptress around. Finally, the baseball coach, who also had brought us a state championship, and whose beautiful and adoring wife was a popular primary teacher, flipped for a high school student whose father was on the school board. Fortunately, this disaster took place long after we left.

Generally, I do not advise superintendents to form close personal relationships with board members, but we became good friends with the Hatfields (cousin of Senator Mark Hatfield). They were older, but not that much, and we really enjoyed each other's children. Their large sheep (and deer) ranch provided an escape from the office – for hunting, picnics and television. They were among the first in this mountainous region to receive the snowy but fascinating pictures which were already common in the East. We rolled up many miles going to their house for the Army/McCarthy hearings. When we mentioned the Hatfield ponies, our boys were ready to head that direction at the drop of a hat. Some of our picnics took place at the ranch of the older Hatfields, who had an interesting custom – when the new Chevrolet model was released each year, grandpa Hatfield would be one of the first to buy a four door sedan. He would take Grandma

Hatfield Ranch

and the grandchildren for a leisurely ride through the hills, and would then jack the new car up on blocks in the garage, leaving it shiny new for exactly a year. Now it was time to drive the new/old Chevy coming off the blocks. We were not clear on the reasoning behind this ritual, but it worked for him.

Allen's World War Two loot included two Mauser rifles. He allowed me to take one to Oregon so that we would have meat for the table. The eight millimeter ammunition was foreign to us, but I was able to buy twenty rounds, which sounded like a lot of venison. I invested a few rounds to zero in the sights, but I had not expected to waste most of the shells in a shooting gallery. Actually, it was a box canyon, and when we puffed over the ridge, we were amazed to see four beautiful bucks grazing far below. Three guns blazed away, but each time we pulled the trigger, a shot from another gun would cause our targets to change direction, resulting in a series of clean misses. Back at the house, our wives heard the impressive fusillade with mixed feelings – always glad to have the venison, they still felt compassion for the graceful creatures, and they also knew who would do much of the preparation. When we walked in with red faces and empty hands, they laughed like crazy.

After lunch, I was dispatched to the top of a small mountain while the Hatfields worked the oak groves from the bottom. With only two cartridges remaining, I found myself staring at a fine six point specimen trotting along the ridge. (In local parlance, he was a three pointer, but I am writing this in New York, and the eastern trophy system sounds more impressive). Given my golden opportunity, I made the classic greenhorn mistake of underestimating the considerable speed of my target. One bullet missed and the other struck his hind quarter, stopping him but leaving him very much alive and well armed with sharp horns and hooves. Far above the treeline, I had not a stick or stone, not even a knife (probably a good thing FOR ME). Lacking the zeal to face him hand to hoof, I took a mighty swing, finishing both the deer and the rifle.

With the horns providing a good handle, and a steep downhill course on dry grass, it was no problem to get my trophy off the mountain, but I never lived down the story of the greenhorn's hunt. The Hatfields retold the tale whenever deer hunting was mentioned anywhere in Oregon.

When I confessed to Allen, he was most gracious (perhaps speechless?) I thought it to be a nice gesture when I gave him a walnut stock blank so that his remaining barrel could better withstand the rigors of the chase. At that time, I had no appreciation for the patience required to work black walnut. I cannot recall that he ever again offered to lend me a shooting iron.

My administrative education included the realization that there are actually parents who physically and sexually abuse their children. Unfortunately, there was no alternative home for the teenage girl who reported a sexually abusive father. She quietly informed him that she knew how to use her deer rifle, and we learned of no more problems. Another family objected strenuously that their daughter was required to walk to a close neighbor's home to catch the school bus. Within the week, the child came to school with badly burned fingers as punishment for telling a fib about the bus stop. I struggled to understand that the parents actually did love their daughter, but had been raised themselves with the finger-burning punishment.

Teacher unions had not reached the rural Northwest, so the procedure at budget time was for the superintendent to recommend and defend individual salaries to the board. I would then hold a faculty meeting to announce the average increase, and I was genuinely surprised the first time a teacher suggested, without emotion, that it would be nice if they were consulted before the fact. On the next cycle, I persuaded the board to agree to a range of salary expenditure, reported the lower end to the principals, listened to their input on individuals and the pool (the total amount available for raises), reported the ball park situation to the faculty, heard their input, and made final recommendations to the board.

Thirty Day School

The schools made progress, and the board rewarded me, though not as well as assumed by the boozy little newspaper correspondent who regularly adorned my office with her huge fruit and flower hats. When I answered her query on my salary, she smiled wickedly and said, "That is the part that shows." I was dumbfounded until she explained that her husband was a retired General Motors executive, and she assumed that all administrators lived on their kickbacks.

My secretary was attractive, innocent and extremely limited in skills. She would try to protect me from pests, but I found it easier to put up with them than to dig my way out of her excuses on my behalf. The daughter-in-law of a board member, she cemented my aversion to

110

nepotism in any form, even though I had accepted help at the Clinton County courthouse (in Frankfort, Indiana). Later, I was invited to interview for principalship of the laboratory school at the University of Illinois, then uninvited when I told them Rupert was my brother. He was not even aware that I was being considered, but I thought the Illinois law was proper.

Another regular office visitor was a mud fence homely mother who was also a teacher, and probably a pretty good student. She brought endless ideas for improving the schools, and one out of 100 was a good idea. A teaching job was never mentioned, and Peggy was convinced that she had a crush on me.

Our splendid gymnasium prompted interest in a town basketball team. Before professional basketball became a huge business, many of the best college players were hired by corporations who then gave them time to represent the firm in AAU (Amateur Athletic Union) leagues. In communities without large corporations, they simply had a town team. Growing up in a Hoosier town which was truly basketball crazy, I did not think of myself as an athlete, only playing a bit in a church league.

Glide had two coaches who were still in good shape, a tree-tall forest ranger, and a number of loggers who were better suited to football than basketball. I tried out for the team, and was surprised to find myself playing most of the time. Our high school basketball coach turned out to be the natural leader of the team, and our employment relationship just might have had some bearing on my acceptance on the team. He was a fabulous passer, and while faking to the other forward, he whipped the ball under the basket where he knew I would be. I practiced handling his bullets so that when he was not connecting with his excellent set shots, I frequently got credit as top scorer instead of Jack. If basketball had counted assists, like hockey, he would have been miles ahead.

The real moment of glory came when we beat the team which beat the team which beat the world AAU champions. No, the keyboard did not stutter. The perennial champion Phillips Oilers lost to a Portland team which then lost to Roseburg Lumber. We were not in Roseburg's league in either respect, but they wanted to play in our gym. I had the ball deep in the corner when my defender, (who started for OSC the previous season) dared me, by body language, to shoot. Both his challenge and my calling his bluff were bad basketball, but I let fly and somehow scored. He was chagrined, and we squeaked out a win, making history but proving nothing, especially when you add the factor of home town officiating for any team, let alone the TOWN TEAM.

Four years passed in an instant, and I realized that I should get back to the doctor's degree. My full year of notice was intended to permit a first class search for a replacement, but it was a mistake. I was a lame duck for too long, and some board members were hurt to think that I would leave after they had treated me so well. They had almost doubled my salary to $9500, and told me that if I would stay, they would even match the stratospheric $10,000 then earned by some of the larger city superintendents.

CHAPTER NINE – THE TOWN THAT FORD BUILT

Returning to the University of Oregon in 1956, we had some modest savings, a fellowship and determination not to leave this time without the doctorate. During the summer, before we moved, I had received a letter from Dean Jacobson informing me of my nomination for the Shankland Award of AASA, the national organization for school superintendents. After dinner, I went back to the office to reread the letter. With hundreds of universities offering education programs, how many nominations would I be up against? With all I faced in winding up my job and moving, should I take time to fill out this endless application, including my complete life history, philosophy and future hopes? I actually tossed the paper, then retrieved it from the waste basket and started writing. Hours later, I mailed the application and forgot it. After many weeks, a surprise phone call announced that I was one of two honorees that year, and should plan to attend the February conference for the presentation in Atlantic City Convention Hall.

We rented another U-Haul truck, moved our belongings to a decent two-bedroom university house and enrolled the boys in school. An incident at that time illustrates the determination Phil has always shown when really wanting to do something. We had bought a pogo stick (probably because I had always been fascinated by them) and the steady Oregon rain required that I reassure Peggy our tiny house would survive our trying out the new toy indoors. Phil quickly sensed that control was better while moving forward, so he started circling our kitchen/dining table to see how long he could maintain balance without a break. He was proud, but a bit wounded when Peggy forcibly ended his marathon after well over 1000 consecutive jumps while still five years old.

I began work on a dissertation proposing the ideal formula for distribution of state school funds. One day the Dean saw me passing his office, and invited me to tell him how things were going. I mentioned being invited to Highland Park, Michigan, to interview for the high-school principalship, but of course, had declined because of my commitments at the University. Without a word, he swivelled to his phone and called Dr. Jim Bushong, superintendent at Grosse Pointe, Michigan. Jim had been at Bend when I was at Sisters, then finished his doctorate and landed one of the best jobs in education. From

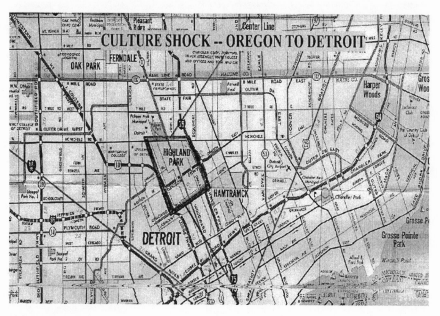

Grosse Pointe, he went to the presidency of the legendary Kamehameha School, which owns much of Honolulu.

Dean Jacobson said only, "Jim, will you call the folks in Highland Park and tell them Evans was temporarily insane, but will be there for the interview?"

Then in the throes of sweeping racial change, now complete, Highland Park had been one of the lighthouse districts in American education, with the first school psychiatrist, first nursery school, etc. Home of the original Ford factory, employees earning a revolutionary minimum of five dollars per day, comparably well paid executives, plus Chrysler headquarters and another major corporation, the city of 50,000, completely surrounded by Detroit, always had a sumptuous tax base and school budget. The good Dean was not going to allow me to miss this opportunity.

I was interviewed by a throng of school board members, administrators, union representatives and civic leaders at a dinner where I was supposed to enjoy a heavy meal while answering nonstop loaded questions. One asked my impression of the school district. I answered honestly that I was tremendously impressed by their reputation and programs, but they appeared to have been living on past glory and momentum for some time. During my return flight, I reflected that I had surely talked myself out of any chance, even if they had been serious about someone as young as thirty.

In a few days, I had an offer of $12,000 plus moving expenses. I hated to trash the dissertation (financial data stale quickly and I had lost a master's thesis this way), but this was big money and prestige at that time. We were able to buy a nice three bedroom Dutch colonial across from Chrysler headquarters for only $9,500 and low taxes. Moving from the mountain air and empty space of Oregon to the sooty snow of Detroit in December was a true culture shock for Peggy, and we have never been certain of the effect on the boys. All school buildings had indoor pools, good libraries, fine musical programs and competent faculties. Elementary enrollment was divided almost evenly between black and white, but staff was almost lily white. One of my first challenges was to convince the Irish head custodian of the high school that we really needed to add a black cleaner, and then to help him succeed on the job. The head man, of course, had not an ounce of prejudice, but he was "worried about his men." We later went through exactly the same dance in hiring the first woman custodian.

Most of us are prone to think of a racially changing community in terms of deteriorating housing, high crime rates and white flight. That was not the case in Highland Park as we saw it, largely because there had been a racial mix for half a century, the rate of change was slow, and the in-migrants were largely middle class. I joined the very strong

Rotary Club and found a proud group of leaders including Stanley Kresge, who was still making money pre-Wal-Mart, and Dr. Hal Stubbs, who incredibly had been successful as a teacher, engineer, lawyer and medical doctor, saving enough money in each stage to finance his education for the next career. Kresge was a member of the downtown Detroit club, but found it more convenient to attend our meetings. He taught me one of life's important lessons: when pie is served with lunch, eat the pie first, because you may then get a second piece.

Guilt was my main feeling at the Atlantic City presentation, even though it was a genuine spectacle. I was on the cavernous stage in a building larger than anything ever imagined, visiting with the top figures of American education arrayed in formal dress. U.S. Commissioner of Education Lawrence Derthick asked me a number of questions, and invited me to apply for a position as his assistant. I thanked him for the compliment, but explained that we had barely unpacked in Highland Park. The program began, and I kept thinking that Peggy had stayed behind with two little boys just recovered from old fashioned measles. Eric then came down with scarlet fever and kidney disease. I wished desperately that Peggy had been able to share this honor which she had earned with me.

When Spring came, we decided to help the boys get out of the city on weekends by buying a boat and joining a little marina with the presumptuous name of Cass Lake Yacht Club. The second-hand fourteen-foot outboard had been out of the water for some time, and we did some bailing during our maiden voyage around Cass Lake. We returned the following morning to find the slip empty and the boat apparently stolen until we saw it resting on the lake bottom. Our next few weekends were spent in caulking and painting, finally producing a decent boat with which we all learned and enjoyed water skiing. The old twenty-five horsepower Mercury was much more powerful than current motors of the same rating, and it towed us at a good clip. Pulling my younger brother, Philip, was something else, because he always fought a weight problem. Once he was up on the skis, we

116

moved right along, but I feared that we would dislocate his shoulders while he was learning to get up. When the Mercury needed help, I took it to a mechanic on Cass Lake. He seemed competent, but lighted a torch right next to a vat of solvent which flared and severely burned his hands and arms. I rushed him to the hospital in my car, and I felt badly that he was hurt while working on my motor.

Blythe's X Car

We later moved up to a larger used boat which we trailered completely around Lake Huron. Our most exciting experience was going through the locks at Sault St. Marie alongside a Great Lakes ship hundreds of feet long. Looking far up to the deck of the freighter, we realized that it could crush us like an eggshell against the stone walls of the lock.

Boating was fun and the boys became pretty good water skiers, but I suspect that on most weekends, they would have preferred to stay in town and play alley basketball.

The family's adjustment was greatly helped by the nearby presence of my Aunt Helen, Uncle Blythe Jones and children, Austin, Suzanne, and Sylvia. Blythe had an excellent position with the Ethyl Corporation, and frequently entertained business guests in their upscale home. We were many times treated to steak and lobster at his huge center-grill tiled table, when this was simply not within our lifestyle. In one period, Blythe drove a miniature car which the Ethyl Corporation was using to test a new kind of transmission. At that time, most of us still used "stick shifts." Another fun part of his work was liaison with the Indy 500 race. I think I was the only family member who never got around to accepting his invitation for a day in the pits of the great race.

After my first year, Dr. Carl Robinson joined the team as business administrator, and we found ourselves frequently allied in battles over educational policy. Our families also had much in common, and we have stayed close, though Carl is gone like so many of our contemporaries. His career path after Highland Park was similar to mine, including superintendencies in New Jersey and Connecticut, and the Vice-presidency of Western Connecticut State. We shared many delightful visits at their Adirondack camp and their retirement home on Jekyll Island.

Our superintendent, Dr. Carlyle Hoyt, had reorganized the large high school in Fairfield, Connecticut, into smaller units imitating the advantages of small schools. He was anxious for me to do the same thing in Highland Park, where we had a huge building shared

Robinson Sixth Lake Camp

with the oldest junior college in Michigan. I took this on as my major goal, and used it for the topic of my second writing of a doctoral dissertation (after also writing a second Master's thesis due to the first interruption of my graduate program). Faculty of the high school were not terribly enthusiastic, correctly sensing that the house plan was more the superintendent's idea than mine. Dr. Hoyt was more feared and respected than liked. His stiff bearing and formal speech made him come across as an elite easterner, and he was not loved for driving a Porsche to work in the automobile capital of America. Old timers also wondered what would happen to their private territory, from favored teaching assignments to the status of the high school as a basketball power.

After visiting Fairfield and other high schools using a house plan, I determined that it was indeed a good theory, and I gradually won over my associates. The toughest to sell were those closest to me, my two assistant principals. They were extremely comfortable, Luke with his long time role as the enforcer, and Ann in her leadership of guidance and activity functions.

Luke always shuddered and shook his head when I scheduled a faculty meeting or called a student assembly. He would have preferred to limit any gathering of faculty or students to a maximum of about three bodies. Faculty meetings were indeed interesting challenges, with the principal facing about 110 union members, and defending actions of the central office as well as my own and my assistants. However, my debating instincts always came through, and I actually enjoyed the exchanges. Luke always whispered on the way out, "I wouldn't have your job for love or money."

Student assemblies were even more disturbing to him, because I would speak frankly about rumors of racial trouble, which he felt would surely trigger the Holocaust – "I wouldn't have your job....." Yet during our four year stay, Highland Park was one of very few high schools in the metropolitan core to avoid any significant racial problems. Both of my assistants, most of the faculty, and most of the elementary principals lived in white neighborhoods of Detroit and northern suburbs, commuting to Highland Park, which was near the epicenter of the bloody race riots at the beginning of World War Two. This surely had some influence on their feelings toward their black students, though almost all of our staff were highly professional.

The most traumatic moment, week, period, of my career came with a call from the athletic department that a young black boy had just been pulled from the men's swimming pool, which was located well down

119

the length of the building toward the junior college. I ran through the many turns of the hallway and down the stairs into the pool area where they were still trying resuscitation. Today's methods might have made a difference.

After dinner, I walked the half a dozen blocks to tell the boy's family how sorry I was. They seemed deeply appreciative that I came to their home. Walking back, I kept hearing the solemnly beautiful passages of Ravel's classic, *Pavane for a Dead Infant*. Next morning, I asked the department head when he and the boy's teacher planned to pay their respects. From his expression, I knew that he had no intention of facing the family, and I gave him only seconds to change his mind.

How could such an accident have happened when swimming teachers are indoctrinated to use the buddy system at all times? We never found an answer. I felt a sense of guilt until time and rationalization eventually provided relief, but from that incident came an insistence on checking and rechecking safety procedures in any organization where I held responsibility.

Reporting to Luke was a functionary entirely new to my experience – a pistol packing plainclothes security officer. Dan was a tough cookie, a veteran of the years of union organizing and union-busting in the automobile industry. Together, they ruled the miles of hallways, though they always deferred to me to pass sentence on guilty students. At a near mob scene following a tense basketball game, neither was in sight when I waded into the middle of the crowd, much to the dismay of my wife.

Many friends have clucked sympathetically when contemplating my years in a racially changing city, but it was not that bad. The boy who hit another student with half a brick, quickly protesting that he had really aimed at the teacher, was the exception, not the rule. Knives frequently were confiscated, but rarely used. When an older girl pulled a knife on Eric, however, it was unsettling to Peggy, but both boys quickly learned that there are good and bad of all races. My work was consuming and generally stimulating, so I did not fully appreciate the strain on Peggy until we left.

Observation, evaluation and follow up with classroom teachers clearly should be the most important part of the principalship, but it also is essential simply to be seen continually and widely. One of my ceremonial functions was the judging of the annual Betty Crocker cherry pie contest. I have no more favorite food, but even a tiny sliver from each of about twenty-five entries can be a bit much. Guess what Peggy had baked to surprise me on the day of the contest!

One of our English teachers continually frustrated his department chairperson with his weak classroom discipline. In December, I tried to work with him, telling him that he should call a timeout with his classes, clearly lay out rules for classroom management, and then ask for administrative backing when the first student flagrantly violated the rules. On the first school day of the new calendar year, he did not appear for class, and we had to find a substitute. Later that day, I received a picture postcard of a beautiful Florida beach with this message, "I was walking on the beach and thought to myself, why not just keep walking?"

My routine was to come home barely in time for dinner, then immediately go to bed with my electronic secretary. Conserving energy in the horizontal position, I dictated text for my dissertation while Peggy slept. During the day, she typed the required five carbon copies of the dissertation which was spread out on the dining table for months. One evening she was terrified to see water dripping through the dining room ceiling when one of the boys left the shower curtain outside the tub. Somehow, the drips missed all of our precious paper.

When the dissertation was finally finished and I was ready for my comprehensive oral exam, we took our longest vacation ever, and drove to Oregon with the boys. In our usual mode of travel gluttony, we included Black Canyon, Bryce, Zion, Grand Canyon, Hoover Dam and Las Vegas, where Eric converted all possible assets to silver dollars which were just ready to disappear from circulation. We simply were not smart enough to seek out the scarcer dates and better condition coins which would soon escalate in value.

Next, we did Southern California, Yosemite and the sequoias, San Francisco and the Pacific Coast to Oregon. The boys had been nearly perfect for the whole long drive, but they missed the tallest tree in the world by ignoring my warning to settle down. We revisited our old home in Glide and stayed at the Hatfield ranch. In the middle of the night before defending my dissertation, we were awakened by a thunderous explosion. A tractor trailer full of dynamite had been parked on a street in Roseburg, and was detonated by a paint store fire, virtually leveling the business district. Aline Hatfield's father lived a mile from the blast and all of his windows were shattered. He was hospitalized and died in a few days.

Despite the disturbance and loss of sleep, I found the examining professors supportive and complimentary, and my hours-long written exam probably was easier for me than for the readers. We quickly got on our way home, again stopping at every possible national park.

Walter Reuther was our commencement speaker one year, and when Dr. Hoyt and I followed him to the stage, Peggy heard someone in the audience speculating that we must be bodyguards. We scarcely looked the part, but there definitely were bodyguards all around him. His number two man was Brendan Sexton, whose wife was a probationary English teacher. When it was time for the big decision, our English department chairlady insisted that Mrs. Sexton should not have tenure, but Luke and others questioned whether we wanted to stomp the toes of a high ranking labor leader. In visiting with her, I asked whether she really enjoyed teaching high school students. She freely admitted that she hated it and offered her resignation, thus avoiding my difficult decision. On a plane trip a couple of years later, my seat mate on one leg of the trip was Gordie Howe, probably the greatest hockey player of all time. On the return trip, my seat mate was Patricia Sexton, who had distinguished herself in writing for higher education.

CHAPTER TEN – HEALTH, HISTORY AND HORSES

When we were called away from a rare and delightful vacation at Higgins Lake for an interview in Saratoga Springs, N.Y., we had absolutely no knowledge of the city. However, we were all curious, so we set out by car to have a look. Reading had told us that Saratoga had the oldest thoroughbred race track in America, and Skidmore College, but little more. The salary was just better than my pay as principal and assistant superintendent, but it was my first chance at a significant

SARATOGA'S UNITED STATES HOTEL
(Smaller than the Grand Union, the world's largest, which boasted a dining room seating one thousand)

superintendency. The board at Cherry Creek, Colorado, had spent a fortune in visiting Highland Park and flying me to Denver, but they had neglected to tell me whether I had received the position. (At

AASA a few years later, I met the other unsuccessful finalist, and he reported also having been left in the dark by the prestigious district.)

Although not announced until later, the other finalist at Saratoga was the long time Deputy in New York City, eventually becoming Chancellor, who had wanted to return to his boyhood home. After my appointment, he gave me a tour of the infamous Livingston Street headquarters and confessed that the NYC schools were ungovernable. (Bernie Donovan did retire to Saratoga and I knew him through Rotary. He served his hometown well in a host of volunteer roles.)

Saratoga had just gone through religious warfare centering on the issue of sex education. The superintendent had been fired by the heavily Catholic board, but they were desperately anxious for peace, and my Protestantism may actually have been an asset. Another hot issue was ability grouping, and my interviewers obviously found it easier to explore this subject than to talk about sex education.

On a second trip without the family, I signed a contract and bought a house without Peggy seeing it. This was dangerous, and the house needed a great deal of work, but she forgave me when she realized it was a wonderful residential street. We had fifty children, largely from professional families, within one block. Out of many splendid neighbors, Bill Tarrant was exceptional. Severely crippled by polio and almost totally blind, he functioned extremely well as head of a factory making equipment for handling snow, leaves, and trash. When Peggy and I were away, the furnace repairman was called, and he forgot that he had left the water fill valve open. When water from the upstairs radiators came through the living room ceiling, Bill was called for help. Despite his handicaps, he diagnosed and fixed the problem, and the mess helped accelerate our renovations.

Board Chairman Charles LaBelle was counsel to the New York State Police, then counsel to the state Conservation Department, and past county chairman of the dominating Republican Party. When I asked him to fill me in concerning community expectations, he said, "You are a big boy, but I hope you stay away from these two outfits: the New England Congregational Church and the Saratoga Golf and

124

Polo Club." We could not begin to afford the time or money for a country club until much later, but we did visit the Congregational Church in making the rounds of all Protestant churches. Music and thought provoking sermons are very important to us. The Congregational Church had the best choir, largely thanks to the tenor President of Skidmore, Val Wilson, and the soprano voice professor, Ruth Lakeway. The sermon was outstanding. We returned for second and third visits, when the minister, Carl Voss called with a friendly warning, "This is the point where I am supposed to give you the membership pitch, but if you are smart, you will look elsewhere." Carl was painfully aware that he had been a lightning rod in the Holy War, and did not want me to get off to a bad start. We thanked him and joined his church anyway. In my four year tenure, I never heard the slightest repercussion, though Charlie surely bit his tongue.

Politics had played a large role in the school system. After only a few weeks, Charlie called about a custodian opening, hoping that we could help a good party worker who was down on his luck. I said his recommendation would be important, other things equal, and checked out the applicant with John LeRoux, assistant superintendent for business, a good Catholic and party activist. When I called Charlie back, I told him that people whose judgment he clearly valued assured me the man had serious drinking and other problems, and had not been able to hold any position. Charlie said, "Oh," and never made another political recommendation. Fortunately, the whole board had been involved in soul searching studies of good boardsmanship with their consultant, Dick Lonsdale, from Syracuse University. This permitted the Vice chairman to innocently bring the board back to their solemn vows whenever they began to stray.

While reconciling polar factions on the issue of ability grouping with one hand, my paramount charge and challenge was to somehow achieve the consolidation of the twenty-two districts then sending students to Saratoga Springs High School,. Many efforts had been made over the years and Saratoga was the largest remaining unconsolidated district in New York. The rural districts mistrusted the wicked city which had been a target of the major gambling crackdown leading to fame for Thomas E. Dewey. Besides, some districts were making money by paying unrealistically low tuition instead of operating their own schools. Consolidation would quadruple the tax rate in one district, triple the rate in another, and double the taxes of the largest district, one of five within the city limits, but outside the city school district. The state education department was ready to scrap its master plan and approve a ring district around but not including the city. This is exactly what happened with Glens Falls, only a few miles to the north. Fortunately, the two old time (regional) District Superintendents sharing jurisdiction for the area, liked what they had seen of the reformed board and me, and they advised the state to let me have one more try with their help.

First, I visited the various small operating schools in the outlying districts to convince the teachers that they would be better off in the enlarged district. I asked them to identify the conditions which kept them from doing their jobs, and I took pictures of those conditions. Along with these color slides, I developed my own charts and graphs into a dog and pony show which I presented whenever and wherever two or more voters might be willing to listen. I tried to tell the truth: that the children of the region were facing a crisis in school quality, especially at the high school level; that the necessary classrooms were unattainable without the bonding capacity of the enlarged district; and although we would build as economically as possible, there would inevitably be tax increases for most families. I showed to the penny what the estimated tax rates would be, and we delivered as promised.

District Superintendents Don Myers and Clayton Brown helped me identify and recruit major taxpayers in each district willing to raise their own taxes for the sake of the kids. Charles and Phyllis Dake hosted a meeting of this core group in their home, and set the pattern by volunteering their support and assistance. Although their home was in a district which would not have a tax increase, their chain of convenience stores, milk and ice-cream plants would pay substantially higher taxes.

126

Before we could schedule the election, I needed cooperation from the State Education Department in revising the master plan so that several neighborhoods could be annexed to other districts where they logically belonged. When the election finally took place, consolidation carried in every single district, and the overall margin was over three to one.

There was no time for relaxation or congratulation, because we had to go through the same grueling process to vote bonds for the crucially needed high-school. At this point, the board passed another test. The leading law firm, with offices in City Hall, had received the sizeable commissions for previous bond issues, and almost everyone assumed that they would again reap the benefits. One of the deceased

Hall of Springs

principals in the firm had been the absolute boss of county politics for many years, and another had been the longtime congressman from the area. The commission would be about $40,000, yet most of the real work would be done by bond specialists in New York City. A lawyer who had worked hard for the consolidation made an offer that the board could not refuse: for $15,000, he would do the bond work in addition to all other school legal requirements for a period of three years. The community finally began to believe that the schools really were and should be above politics.

Using the same volunteers and techniques employed for consolidation, the bond issue also passed by a lopsided margin. In order to build the necessary classrooms within our still limited bonding capacity, the architects developed a campus plan. Some parents never did understand why we were limited to $2.6 million for construction, and they complained until more generous budgets made it possible for one of my successors to enclose the covered walkways from the winter blast of Northern New York. On several occasions, I heard strangers talking about the idiots who built the high school, but they simply did not know how lucky we were to get the job done at all.

One big hurdle was the quiet accumulation of the minimum acreage for a school site within walking distance of any significant proportion of students. We needed to ask Monsignor Burns if he would trade an undeveloped portion of the dedicated Catholic cemetery for an equal amount of land at the other end of his property. This came on the heels of the sex education fuss and the necessity to raise taxes on the largely Catholic residents of the city. Again, it was convenient to have a board who were mostly Catholics, and the good Monsignor came through.

Peggy and the boys were soon accepted by their peer groups in Saratoga. Both boys were good athletes, which sped their adjustment. Peggy's friendly and open manner has made her an immediate "native" wherever she has gone.

The city had deteriorated from its nineteenth-century splendor, but was beginning to regenerate. Several civic leaders (including our new friends Charles and Philly Dake, and Newman and Jane Wait) supported a performing arts center in a natural bowl at the Saratoga Spa State Park originally sponsored by Simon Baruch, then developed by Governor Franklin D. Roosevelt. Current Governor Nelson Rockefeller signed on to the plan with both personal and state funds. From that moment, SPAC has been a continuing success story, and Saratoga has gone nowhere but up. The Philadelphia Orchestra and New York City Ballet have their summer homes here, along with the Lake George Opera and world class chamber music and dance groups. We also have the National Museum of Racing and the National Museum of Dance.

Newman "Pete" Wait was president of the local bank and my doubles tennis partner. We appeared to be losing in the finals of the county tournament, when Pete started rolling on the court in pain from leg cramps. Our opponents generously took time out to pound on his calf with a racquet, got him on his feet and watched helplessly as we took over the momentum of the match and won. Bill Dake still claims it was a carefully planned fraud.

We had been in Saratoga exactly one year when a board member called from Highland Park to ask if I would return as superintendent, This was flattering, but not tempting despite a financial package nearly double what I was making (the big payoff would have been in the pension). I explained that it would not be fair to my new district, where I was just getting started in the consolidation effort. The board member said that if I was concerned about our children living in the city, we could live in the Birmingham area and send the boys to the Cranbrook School. What would you think of a superintendent's commitment if he and his children were too good to live in the school district?

A continuing source of stress was the determination of a board member to have his son appointed as a high school teacher. I explained that while he was a fine candidate, and might win if it came to a legal test, the appointment would undermine the recently earned credibility of the board. Under New York law, a board cannot make an appointment except by recommendation of the superintendent, so our board members were spared the difficult decision as to whether they would support me or a fellow member. All they could do was to fire me. I never asked for one of the currently popular contracts providing for just cause or indemnity. To his credit, the proud father never proposed my firing. He was stubborn, but fair.

As a life member of the National Education Association, I still held one office in the New York State Teachers Association, though it was already apparent that administrators could no longer feel welcome in an organization struggling against the AFT to become the dominant teacher union. My office was that of chairman of the Ethics Committee. I was dismayed by the emerging pattern of teachers and administrators accepting payment for their endorsement of everything from chalk to school buses, and I took this on as a personal crusade. When the past President of our New York superintendents association appeared in a full page ad in a national journal, I wrote both to him and the magazine editor that I would appreciate their leadership in helping to stop such endorsements. Fortunately I had found an old administrative code of ethics specifically banning such endorsements, and there was no evidence that it had been repealed or amended. Both men immediately agreed with my position, and there was almost instant cessation of the ads, although I have seen a few in recent years.

The endless night meetings and campaigning took their toll. When I quit running on adrenalin, my body got even by succumbing to a retarded case of mononucleosis at age thirty-four. Liver involvement helped to keep me in bed for seven weeks. Months earlier, Skidmore President Wilson had recommended me to Rensselaer Polytechnic Institute President Folsom, who had asked for leads for the vacancy of Vice-President for student affairs. President Folsom had waited patiently for me to schedule a group interview with administrators, faculty representatives and student leaders. He suggested a cocktail party in the President's mansion. My neighbor and friend, Dr. Bill Meinhardt, reluctantly agreed, with the provision that I take it easy and drink no more than a single beer. It turned out to be a stand up affair, and I was backed up to the fireplace for several hours of good-natured grilling while Peggy suffered from a distance.

Shortly after my arrival in Saratoga, a new reporter mistakenly attributed to me a quotation actually made by the board chairman, strongly stating that policy on ability grouping should be left strictly to the superintendent. The board and I had been told that negative press is best ignored, so we bit our tongues. On the second morning, an editorial blasted me for being self-serving. This time, I visited the editor. He apologized, but said I should have spoken up. I survived, and he became a strong supporter of the consolidation, the bond issue, and me personally. When I resigned for the RPI position, his editorial headline was, "BOARD NEEDS ANOTHER DR. EVANS." I felt well repaid for the earlier editorial wound.

CHAPTER ELEVEN – RPI – TURBULENT YEARS

Rensselaer Polytechnic Institute, the oldest and one of the most distinguished technological universities in the nation, is within commuting distance of Saratoga, so my transition to the new job was made easier in some respects, but harder in others. I continued to have many evening commitments, and I had been spoiled by virtually no commuting in my previous work. Before long, we bought a house near Shaker High School, across the river from RPI, making it possible for me to attend both our sons' activities and those at RPI, sometimes totaling thirty or more games, plays and concerts in a week. Eric and Phil were pretty good athletes, and when they were on the same basketball team, they were undefeated in the regular season.

RPI Council

My position certainly had variety and challenge. First called director of student affairs until I proved myself, then Vice-President (eventually becoming V.P. and Vice Provost to legitimize my authority as a non-faculty member dealing with faculty problems), I was responsible for undergraduate admissions and financial aid, graduate ditto, registrar, Dean of students, health services, counseling services, placement office, physical education, athletics, sometimes alumni affairs, and standing in for the President whenever and wherever he or anyone else requested.

This variety gave me considerable freedom of movement and action as long as I kept on top of everything. Before I finally tired of the long days commuting to New York City, I was able to include many interesting people and places along with the mandatory stops. A regular duty was the delivery and presentation of Rensselaer fifty-year pins (studded with tiny rubies) to alumni too old, too angry, too far away or too disinterested to visit the campus. This was always enjoyable, sometimes truly enlightening to discover what our alumni had done with their lives. Only one third had actually practiced engineering or science, but virtually all were glad they had received the rigorous training which many hated at the time.

Even those who were angry softened enough to invite me, and many times Peggy, to stay for refreshments, and some even renewed their association with the school. A few invited us to stay with them and kept in touch for years.

During my very first month, Dean of Students Ira Harrod convinced me that two of our fraternities were fragrantly dead and deserved burial. When I gave this news to the President, he told me this would be an excellent opportunity for me to meet the board of trustees. What he knew, and I did not, was that the two houses included four alumni who were trustees and had jointly given ninety-five percent of the current gift income to RPI that year. They included J. Erik Jonsson, founder of Texas Instruments, Clay Bedford, chairman of the vast Kaiser Industries and builder of the Liberty Ships which saved England in WW II, and Phil Grove, builder of many huge airports and subways. The trustees made me squirm just a bit with their questions, but they gave their unanimous support for whatever needed to be done. Ironically, they had just donated considerable money to renovate the houses. Phil Grove, who became a good friend and host extraordinaire, often kidded me about the fact that my office ended up in his old bedroom when we converted the Deke House to student affairs offices.

Dekes had a solid reputation for drinking, but the last straw had been a series of some seventeen fires, several of which had been reported by the same brother, whose own bed was the last thing to burn. The Police Chief, Fire Chief and the Deans were all convinced that he must be the guilty person, and the police believed that he failed a lie-detector test. They wanted him out of R P I and Troy pronto. My office was the major level of appeal in our disciplinary process, so when he pleaded innocent, I bluffed a bit by telling him that he could leave without charges being pressed, but if he continued to maintain his innocence, we would be forced to go to a sodium pentothal test which was "virtually foolproof." He surprised me by opting for the test. Now there was nothing I could do except arrange the test through our psychiatrist. He reported back that the student apparently was telling the truth. The enforcement officers were not pleased, and felt that I should have thrown him out with or without solid evidence. I was not about to do so, and the President backed me.

We will never know how the fires started, but the accused student solved his drinking problem, made perfect grades and took a work study assignment with IBM, leading to regular employment.

One of my special assignments was a study suggested by our leading trustee and industrialist, Erik Jonsson, to determine the feasibility of buying the former Skidmore College real estate for an RPI lower division campus. It was assumed that we could educate first and second year students at relatively low cost and increase the cost effectiveness of the upper division programs by feeding in the survivors from Saratoga. Because of my Saratoga connections, this was a labor of love and my first instinct was strongly in favor.

135

Skidmore was almost giving away the property which now brings huge prices since Saratoga has again become the place to live.

My study and reflection, however, resulted in a negative

recommendation. Mr. Jonson himself had challenged the Skidmore board to accept his gift of the 1,000 acre Woodlawn estate, 50,000 shares of Texas Instruments stock and cash for the first building if they would abandon the old campus and start out fresh. This was a daunting and spectacularly successful challenge (not immediately accepted) and its rationale had not changed. The old campus was too small and the buildings were old mansions difficult to heat and maintain.

However, the most powerful reason for rejecting the proposal was the fact that RPI had made its reputation on quality, not quantity, and the number of good risks among our rejectees was not that great.

President Folsom recommended my conclusion to the board, but we both wondered how Mr. Jonsson would feel about it. He was also a trustee at Skidmore, and the project would have relieved them of a white elephant. As usual, Mr. J was a class act. When I drove him from one trustee meeting to the other (on a day when the stock market cost him seventy million dollars without his batting an eye), he congratulated me for a study finding which recognized the wisdom of his own original position. Until his passing, he continued to be RPI's outstanding donor and advisor.

Along with Carroll Folsom, wife of the president, Peggy became known as a hostess extraordinaire on campus. I imposed on her frequently with surprise guests, and each fall, we invited to our house many groups of new freshmen from far away states and countries.

When leaders of industry, education and government came to receive honorary degrees and/or to speak, we and the Wiberleys frequently were called upon to meet airplanes and host the visitors. Instead of tapping the institutional budget and caterers, much of the food was prepared by wives of the president and top staff. However, they enjoyed getting together and had many good laughs. After preparing a huge salad, the wife of the dean of students discovered that a fingernail had been sliced off, and five administrators' wives went searching through the mountain of produce before serving it with prayers that the errant nail would not appear on the plate of a distinguished guest.

A frequent unannounced guest was John Horton, trustee, major donor and tennis partner. As a descendant of the inventor of the Hortonsphere, the water tower which is the first visible landmark in the approach to thousands of small towns and cities, John could afford to experiment with dozens of interesting, if offbeat, enterprises. Included were such polar activities as reintroducing to Third World cultures the old tin washboard (now in fiberglass), and the fitting of deep-diving World War Two submarines with high tech equipment for undersea oil exploration.

If John has faults, pretension is not one of them. More than once, he would appear with a lunch consisting of chocolate milk and a candy bar, bringing them to our table to mix with whatever Peggy had prepared for me. One visit was well announced – he drove his old car into our driveway loudly dragging the entire exhaust train. He somehow got his very robust frame under the car to disengage the wreckage and leave it as a gift.

Another special assignment and challenge for us (and the Wiberleys) was the care and feeding of the RPI relationship with Ellis Robison, owner of a largely nineteenth century wholesale drug company. Even his warm and delightful family would be the first to describe him as crusty, cantankerous and penny-conscious, but with our encouragement, of course, he was most generous to RPI as well as to other universities. I spent many hours helping him grade coins received on approval from major dealers. If only I had heeded his advice to sell all of my "junk" (low grade coins) and buy one coin ranking among the best of its kind, I would be a much wealthier collector today. As an example, I was in his office one day when Harvey Stack, perhaps the top dealer in the country, arrived from New York City. Ellis took us to lunch, where Harvey pulled out of his pocket a rare four-dollar U.S. gold piece with a price of eighteen thousand dollars. Ellis was secretly delighted, but grumbled the price down to fifteen thousand . Within the month, Stack called to unsuccessfully offer thirty thousand. In three months, the value was one hundred thousand. When Ellis finally donated his collection to RPI and Cornell, Stack auctioned that coin for two hundred fifty thousand.

The major sport at RPI was ice hockey. Before my arrival, Ned Harkness had coached the school to national championships in both lacrosse and hockey, even though he had played neither sport. Whenever we had a losing streak, I could count on at least one phone call from a wealthy alumnus asking why we did not bring back Ned. My innocent answer was that we had no vacancy, but would certainly consider Ned if we did. He had gone on to coach Cornell to multiple championships, a brief executive term with the Detroit Red Wings, and management of the Lake Placid Olympic Authority.

I became a hockey fan, and had no problem justifying the generous scholarships for which most players qualified. Every RPI freshman had to be a strong enough student to survive rigorous versions of both calculus and physics, and since most hockey candidates lived in rural Canada, they had a genuine financial need at such an expensive university. For these reasons, I held out against giving purely athletic scholarships. This policy changed after I left, and perhaps helped in winning a second national championship. We will never know.

The kind of financial aid which really sent me on the trail of donors was exemplified in spades when one of our counselors suspected that a boy was having financial problems. In checking with the financial aid office to see if they could give additional help, he was amazed to learn that the student had not even applied for aid. He had thought financial aid was for the poor. His own family owned a hill farm on the Vermont border, where had they had been selling off their little dairy herd a few cows at a time to pay his tuition.

When I first met Dr. Joe Pahl, director of health services, he looked up from his always commanding stature, though under five feet tall., and said, "I understand that you are my new boss, but you won't have to put up with me very long." He was referring to the fact that he was a walking medical textbook, and had been rejected initially by the medical school because of serious heart problems at age nineteen. He could be a tough cookie on behalf of students when dealing with faculty, administration and trustees. Fortunately we were always on the same side, and Peggy and I became close friends with Shirley and Joe. Despite the gloomy introduction forty years ago, he survived until the very writing of this chapter. Surely Shirley (we have made a thousand jokes about her name) has earned her place in heaven. Perhaps she will now learn the pleasure of a full night's rest.

For convenience in assembling the administrative council, the President moved my office back to the administration building, lengthening my commute from a few steps to a half mile. This slight sacrifice was offset by having an office adjoining Steve Wiberley, Vice Provost and Dean of the Graduate School. On many occasions, he had helped keep the administrative council focused on the fact that colleges exist ultimately to serve students, not faculty. We became even better friends, and sometimes with Peggy and Betty, we took interesting trips representing the University at major fund-raisers and at such ROTC training locations as Pensacola and Fort Bragg. On one such trip, we visited his brother at Norris Lake, Tennessee, and jointly bought a cabin. We never spent a night in it, but Al kept it rented for us until someone torched it on Halloween.

Student government was old and highly developed at RPI. Despite the high tuition costs, students were willing to vote a relatively high and mandatory activity fee, which financed a fine new student union building and extensive programs. One of the best was radio station W R P I, which had loyal listeners, to mostly pop music, far beyond the campus and community. One of the three major television stations moved to the Helderberg Mountains and abandoned a 900 foot tower adjacent to the Rensselaer Technology Park, so the students suggested a donation. I had the challenge of formalizing the gift, and inducing the President to accept it. There is more than a little liability involved with students scrambling up a tower of that height, though a fall of 900 feet would not hurt any more than the first 100. Also, there was the matter of raising thousands of dollars for a state-of-the-art FM antenna to effectively utilize the tower. The other clubs recognized this as a unique opportunity for the campus and its image among another 100 miles of pre-college population, so they readily agreed to tighten their own budgets to pay for the antenna and other needed equipment.

Many alumni of the station have gone into successful careers in broadcasting, including the recently retired top anchor of the Capital District. Following my retirement, Peggy and I visited a former WRPI President and two of his former sidekicks who now have an extremely successful business in designing and installing broadcast equipment. He gave us a delightful flight in his twin engine Piper Saratoga, which we all felt was exceedingly appropriate, landing near the beach at Santa Barbara, and walking a short distance to lunch. We were amazed that he was given clearance to fly directly over the huge and busy LAX airport while showing us downtown Los Angeles.

My years in student affairs administration spanned the protest period of the late '60s and early '70s. After only a few years, I was virtually the only such administrator left of the national group I joined in 1964.

During some of the more trying times, my venture outdoors for the morning paper would find me reciting the seminally brief final chapter in Dickens' *Tale of Two Cities*,

"The day of the execution dawned bright and clear."

Of course I survived each day, finally unwinding with a stroll which frequently recalled the Orin Crain classic, "Slow me down, Lord!"

Slow me down, Lord!
Ease the pounding of my heart
by the quieting of my mind.
Steady my hurried pace
With a vision of the eternal reach of time.

Give me,
Amidst the confusion of my day,
The calmness of the everlasting hills.
Break the tensions of my nerves
With the soothing music of the singing streams
That live in my memory.

Help me to know
The magical restoring power of sleep.

Teach me the art
Of taking minute vacations: of slowing down
    to look at a flower;
    to chat with an old friend or make a new one;
    to pat a stray dog;
    to watch a spider build a web;
    to smile at a child;
    or to read a few lines from a good book.

Remind me each day
That the race is not always to the swift;
That there is more to life than increasing its speed.

Let me look upward
Into the branches of the towering oak
And know that it grew great and strong

Because it grew slowly and well.

Slow me down, Lord,
And inspire me to send my roots deep
Into the soil of life's enduring values
That I may grow toward the stars
Of my greater destiny.

O.L. Crain
Eastertime, 1957

RPI was fortunate to avoid the violence and damage suffered by many universities, but this did not come automatically. When our students read about the docility of engineering and science students, this was a challenge to prove that they were not brain-dead. Also, we had departments of humanities and social sciences who felt they should take the lead in arousing the rest of the institution. When campuses everywhere exploded on the occasion of our invasion of Cambodia, hundreds of RPI students protested, and like their brethren elsewhere, needed to occupy an administration building. The smallest and easiest target because of proximity to the student union was the Student Affairs building. In the early morning, they broke a single small glass to unlock a door, and announced to the world that they had occupied an administrative office.

Our home was the former President's residence only yards from my office, so Peggy found herself hostess to the command post for a couple of days. The President allowed faculty leaders to mediate the crisis, and the students soon evacuated, carefully cleaning the building as they left.

Governance issues generally produced only two student camps: activists and a large number of spectators. Virtually no one counter demonstrated to defend board or administrative positions.

With war/political issues, we had a moderate sized but aggressive group of activists, approximately equal numbers of less aggressive counter demonstrators and a large number of spectators. The activists gave me the most grief, yet I had to admire their guts, especially in the earlier demonstrations when they were more likely to be abused as Communists and traitors. Their life was much easier after highly respected citizens and acknowledged patriots began to question the war.

In an interval of a demonstration, I tried to capture the frustration of the demonstrators and scribbled,

VIETRAGEDY

With the best intent, our sons were sent
    to the far end of the world
where they could not know either phantom foe
    or why flags back home soon furled.
So their life blood seeped down that rathole deep
    where the French long since had ceased.
Their epitaph terse was a Kipling verse:
    They tried to hurry the East

Each year brought a different issue, but there were two constants:

1. To each class, I explained the seeming overemphasis on faculty research and publishing compared to the teaching of undergraduates. I conceded that there is pressure on faculty to publish, but contended that there must be exciting interdisciplinary research to maintain faculty quality in a first class institution. Fortunately, I could point to several popular teachers of undergraduates who were respected in academia and well paid by R P I.

2. Each class had capable leaders anxious to share in the governance of R.P.I. My approach to this pool with such great potential for good and bad was lifted straight from teaching practice through the ages: expect and demand of students not what they are today but what they may become.

When a new issue was raised, I would "remind" everyone that RPI had no anarchists, only people who wanted to work within the system to correct our deficiencies. At this point, some would quickly disappear and the others would roll up their sleeves.

To each newly appointed administrator, trustee and faculty officer, I had to demonstrate that student affairs administration was more than keeping the animals caged. The entire university community needed to understand that *big issues usually are small ones which have been mishandled.*

Professor of
Urinalysis

Dean Mochon's Comment on
Specialization

When students care enough to stick their necks out and identify a problem, administrators had better find a way to involve the serious workers in campus wide study and improvement. *Leaders in denial rarely last long.*

An article which I wrote for the *Chronicle of Higher Education,* February 5, 1973, appeared to ring a bell for many readers,

"Critical mass applies to human problems as surely as it governs physical reactions. The misjudging or mishandling of a small problem all too often delivers (to a previously unsuccessful cause) a concentration of dedicated opponents who rise to dangerous energy levels through mutual endocrine reinforcement.

"The key and the challenge, then, is to approach each potential crisis with that rare objectivity that avoids confusing friends and enemies, that avoids delivering toward that critical mass those who would like to remain friendly, or at least uncommitted."

I was stating the obvious, and it probably has been better articulated by others but I surely wish that the second Bush administration had given more attention to the principle.

In that decade, I did not need urging to do something about recruiting women and black students, but I was always in the pressure point between those who felt we were doing too little, and those who liked to pretend, "I'm not prejudiced, but nobody ever gave me any special attention." RPI was actually founded to serve both men and women, and there were a few coeds from 1824 to World War Two. In the fifties, the few women students lived in Russell Sage College dorms and walked up the big hill to classes at RPI. Most thinking people recognized that we were missing out on a huge pool of potential technological talent, and we recruited vigorously. However, the simple fact was that it was not culturally popular for girls to study the required math and science courses, and the same thing was true in inner-city schools serving the majority of black students.

My best single strategy was to reorganize the venerable Rensselaer Medal program for top math/science students, awarding the traditional medal along with a lapel pin and generous scholarship to the top junior in a much larger number of high schools. With this timing, winners were made aware of RPI before their final choice of colleges, and while there was still time to beef up their math and science preparation. It was never easy, but once we began to attract larger numbers of women and blacks, the word was spread and success fed success.

Nevertheless, activists both on and off campus believed anything we might do to be insufficient – token, at best. Privately, student leaders praised our new efforts and hoped we would understand that some of the protests were rituals necessary to demonstrate universal brotherhood. We did understand, but we were shot in the back a few times while leading the charge.

Most demonstrations were strictly local, orderly and becoming of a community of scholars. The more difficult happenings were those national circuits of controversial speakers. Their promoters would ask potential local sponsors if RPI was going to be the only major university whose students were denied the right to hear Mr. X. Of course not!!! – then it quickly became a free speech issue between campus and community. When Eldridge Cleaver came with his retinue of Black Panthers, we were all prepared, though nervous. Within an hour, he had used up his invectives and was gone.

Dr. Timothy Leary, the marijuana/LSD guru, made a bigger splash. We agreed to his appearance only in a debate, facing a physician well known for his writing on the negative effects of the so-called soft drugs. Even with this precaution, which we believed consistent with a university setting, there were many angry alumni and residents. Free speech/assembly issues and the resulting publicity guaranteed a packed fieldhouse with full television and press coverage. The event went smoothly, and some of the angry letters were followed by apologies. Listeners heard only what they wanted to hear, but the few impartial agreed that the overall effect was positive, both for education and for drug control.

Marijuana was not unknown on any campus at that time, and the residence hall counselors would occasionally plant a rumor that the Deans were going to make a sweep, and then they would laugh at the sound of flushing toilets.

Two larger protests concerned governance of the university. One was a disagreement with the perceived lack of Presidential priority for better library facilities. President Richard G. Folsom wanted as badly as anyone else to have a better library, but was unwilling to promise more than we could afford. The happy outcome was greater library support by all parties, with a fine new building named The Folsom Library.

The most serious dispute concerned a Presidential search gone sour. After constructive preliminaries involving faculty, students, trustees and alumni, two finalists were invited to campus to meet an enlarged committee. A poll of the faculty and student representatives revealed that, surprisingly, there was unanimous support for one man, but the subcommittee of trustees announced that the other had been appointed. The trustees' ground rules had stated that any one of the finalists would be assumed to have the support of all groups when the trustees

146

exercised their prerogative of the final decision. The less popular of the two was said to have pressed the trustees for a decision, and they committed to him assuming that any large committee of faculty and students would be unable to agree unanimously on anything.

Five trustees were on campus when the news broke that both faculty and students were outraged. Recalling that a similar incident at a similar university ended with the new Vice hounded from office within months, I asked the trustees present if they would be willing to meet with elected faculty and student leaders to absorb some of the energy.

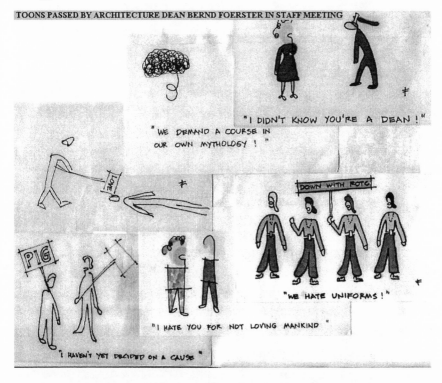

TOONS PASSED BY ARCHITECTURE DEAN BERND FOERSTER IN STAFF MEETING

"I DIDN'T KNOW YOU'RE A DEAN !"

"WE DEMAND A COURSE IN OUR OWN MYTHOLOGY ! "

LOVE

DOWN WITH ROTC

PIG

"WE HATE UNIFORMS !"

"I HATE YOU FOR NOT LOVING MANKIND "

"I HAVEN'T YET DECIDED ON A CAUSE "

They agreed and although the retiring President and three other Vice Presidents were present, I found myself chairing this meeting de facto. The trustees were willing to take the position that if a mistake was made, anger should be directed at them and not at the President-elect. After several hours, the student and faculty leaders agreed with this position, but pointed out that it would not be practical to involve the entire campus in a similar meeting to gradually vent their anger. Though pessimistic, they finally agreed to constitute a "committee for fair play" which would invite the President-elect to an open meeting after careful preparation urging the campus toward open mindedness through hundreds of small group meetings. During the same long night, several plans for overt disruption were discovered and defused.

The multiple small group meetings helped to dissipate the energy so that when the President-elect came to speak from the interior balcony of the student union, the crowd was reasonably respectful. He was a persuasive speaker, though not entirely forthcoming concerning his knowledge of the situation before accepting the appointment. In any event, the crisis passed and the trustees were generous in their compliments to me for handling the problem.

Commencement usually produced at least one surprise, normally not as serious as the stress of waiting to learn what it might be. One year, the activists showed their displeasure with the "military-industrial" speaker by facing their chairs away from the stage. Trustee Irwin Hale, seated in the first row on the stage, turned his chair to face away from the silent protesters. Point and counterpoint both made without disruption, and the university maintained its tradition of free speech.

The graduation programs were a source of much pleasure to me despite the stress. Our distinguished trustees and other alumni made a great effort to attend, and the academic procession was a heart-warming demonstration of the American story of success through education and hard work. Few students have come to Rensselaer from privilege and none for an easy ride.

Our board chairman at that time was Dr. Detlev Bronk, pioneer in bio-physics, President of the National Academy of Sciences and President of Rockefeller University. He was a splendid speaker whose rich bass voice belied his small stature. During one of his speeches when I was seated behind him, I was amazed to realize that he had been standing on tiptoes for nearly an hour in order to be seen above the massive podium. I was the only one in an audience of thousands privy

148

to his painful position. Was it prideful insecurity which, despite his numberless honors, kept him from detaching the mike and assuming a more relaxed position beside the podium?

The new President allowed me to continue defending his performance for five years, but I no longer enjoyed the inner circle. Several top level administrators were fired in the first year. When he finally received the megabuck opportunity in corporate life, the President had the board act on my resignation (which I had offered earlier) just minutes before he announced his own departure.

We left RPI feeling the greatest respect and affection for the old school. Peggy had served as President of the faculty wives and had entertained many hundreds of students, faculty, trustees and alumni. Our farewell reception was well attended, and the gifts of crystal and carved ivory were directed at least as much to Peggy as to me.

Many trustees sent complementary letters thanking us for our service to RPI, and we have stayed in touch with a few (many are no longer living). When national news reported an anonymous gift of 365 million to RPI as being the largest in history to any university, naturally there was much chatter as to the donor. While I would not speculate in public, I decided to have a little fun. In my Christmas note to Sheldon Roberts, I congratulated him for his most generous gift. (Sheldon had been a co-founder of Fairchild Electronics, which was sold to General Electric for considerable stock). Sheldon bounced back immediately with a phone call, protesting "I may have given the school a few million, but I don't have THAT kind of money!" The secret was kept for a couple of years, and when the donor was revealed, it was someone virtually unremembered at RPI, but not surprisingly, he had a Silicon Valley address.

Sheldon and his lovely wife, Pat, were both enthusiastic pilots, so they needed two airplanes for many years. Pat traveled great distances serving as a volunteer judge for university aerobatic competitions. Sheldon preferred to fly his own plane to trustee meetings in New York, from California, then Oregon. Peggy and I sometimes drove him to the Albany airport. We felt terribly guilty seeing him take off into a

149

headwind approaching sixty miles per hour, especially since he had chosen to use the smaller plane on that trip. The Roberts are now living very close to our one-time home on the University of Oregon campus, and recently gave twenty-four sousaphones to establish the University marching band as the absolute leader in the sousaphone department. When they first moved to Oregon, it was to the fly-in community of Sun River, just across the ridge from our former home at Sisters. Sheldon traveled all the way from Oregon to attend my retirement dinner, and at the end of our retirement cruise from Alaska to Vancouver, B.C., we were guests of Sheldon and Pat at Sun River.

CHAPTER TWELVE –BACK TO THE SUPERINTENDENCY

My parachute was neither golden nor silvery, but the University financed a good relocation counseling series in N.Y. City. I was thoroughly tested, led through introspective essays, and appeared to be heading toward corporate middle management. Learning about the superintendent opening in Ithaca, N.Y., I visited my old associate Don Myers in Saratoga County to ask for a recommendation. He said that he would be delighted to help, but if I were serious about going back into public school administration, would I like to gamble a couple of years as his assistant on the chance that I might succeed him. The regional district superintendents in New York are a strange breed, wearing one hat as assistant to the New York State Commissioner of Education, and another hat as executive officer of the regional Board of Cooperative Educational Services, reporting to a board made up of representatives of the component school districts. The Saratoga BOCES included parts of Washington and Warren counties.

Although we had been away for 11 years, we had maintained many friendships in Saratoga. Peggy was delighted at the prospect of returning. I had left the schools in good shape, so my appointment was generally well received, including a complimentary editorial in the local paper. Jane and Pete Wait, President of the home town bank and a leader of many civic groups, held a "Welcome Home" reception. Peggy was quickly voted into the most prestigious women's charitable sorority and soon became one of the early Presidents of the Action Council for the Performing Arts Center.

The only sour note, but one not to be taken lightly, was the complaint by a board member of the largest component school district that no matter how good this Evans is, there should have been an open search before filling the position. Of course, there was a Schenectady newspaper reporter present, and I made a headline, deja vu my experience just after arriving in Saratoga the first time. This time around, the Saratoga paper did not pick up the theme. I made it a point to give that school board every opportunity to question me, and the complaining member ended up as one of my strong supporters.

We considered only houses in our previous neighborhood, and found a good buy only a few blocks away. The neighboring houses are not distinguished, but Virginia Kraft Payson, who married the owner of the New York Mets, bought across the street, at the South end of our block for her employees quarters and her large racing stable, plus land behind us which has only a tiny house and stable. Her riding horses relax across the fence from our deck, and they were joined by a yearling she purchased in the two-week annual Saratoga sale. We were pleased to learn that she named it after our street, Salem Drive, but we did not have enough loyalty or sense to bet on it when it came of racing age. It paid huge odds until the handicappers saw it was a genuine winner. It even brought home $750,000 for losing a race. The sultan of Dubai decided to let the world hear about his tiny country, if only on the sports pages. He invited world class golfers, tennis players, and horse owners to compete in high stakes competition in Dubai, even paying to fly the horses and their training teams to the Middle East.

Some staff probably were skeptical about my transition from higher education back to the public schools, and a State Education Department executive with a major voice in the process had been heard saying it would be a cold day in hell before I was appointed. It was true that the commissioner made the final appointment, but it was his policy to support the recommendation of the BOCES board wherever possible, and it could recommend only from a final list previously approved by him. The board followed the Department procedures, interviewed the finalists, and recommended me to the commissioner, who made the appointment. From this moment, the doubting state officer supported me, and we became good friends.

The commissioner asked me to chair two of his ongoing advisory councils – one dealing with the asbestos problem in school buildings. This was a thankless hot potato because some state officials and some superintendents were still in denial. When we heard testimony from doctors concerning the alarming cancer rate among New York City school custodians, I told the foot draggers privately that they could not expect our defense when they were sued for negligence. The schools were cleaned up fairly quickly from that point.

The other Advisory Council recommended policy on programs for gifted and talented students. The commissioner's choice in this case probably was influenced by the fact that our BOCES had an outstanding program and director of gifted education including a ballet teacher who was still the top ballerina in the nation – Melissa Hayden. This was a happy by-product of the Saratoga Performing Arts Center. Thanks to another local institution, Yaddo, some of our students were mentored by world class writers, composers and artists during their residencies at the former Spencer Trask estate. Our director was Phyllis (husband Alexander Aldrich was a nephew of Governor Nelson Rockefeller) Aldrich, whose energy and contacts opened many doors for our children.

The most memorable meeting of this council took place on a Monday following my return from Hawaii. The phone finally roused me in midmorning with the information that the commissioner and members from all across the state were assembled and were wondering if I planned to attend. Within minutes, I arranged for a surrogate chairman to start the meeting, dressed and hit the road. While driving to Albany, I realized that our 200 mph tailwind and record setting flight from Honolulu to Chicago had left me with jet lag like nothing I had ever known.

BOCES are a New York invention much envied by educators in other states. Funded by a mix of state and local funds depending on the taxable resources of the component districts, they are empowered to offer almost any educational or administrative service which can be performed more efficiently through a consortium of districts.

At the other extreme from gifted programs, we served the handicapped (once called disabled, now challenged), ranging from those who were brilliant, but emotionally disturbed, to the profoundly handicapped who were previously institutionalized at much higher

153

expense. In one case, we created a day program for children who were weekly commuting 200 miles to New York City. Upon arriving at the school for blind and deaf, the paid adult companions would get back on the bus for the upstate home locations, then repeat the process at week's end. Now the children can remain with their families.

Another large component was the vocational/technical program, making high-school students and adults employable in dozens of occupations – massage therapy for the Saratoga Spa State Park, computer programming/operation, forestry, nursing, computer assisted design and machining, etc. etc. – in addition to the traditional trades and food services. In programs having a higher education track, our graduates received a full year of credit at many community and technical colleges.

Other BOCES offer programs unique to their locations, e.g. aircraft maintenance and commercial fishing on Long Island, which is divided into three BOCES. One of the three superintendents became too greedy with his salary and perks, so a new law limits BOCES salaries to a level just below the commissioner. My salary was never that high but the law causes problems in some regions. The natural progression is from the superintendency of the larger and more prestigious local districts to the BOCES. Some of the more affluent communities pay their own superintendents more than either the commissioner or the BOCES superintendent, because the local boards include corporate executives and other well paid professionals

Some services encompass more than one BOCES. In the case of computer services, there is an integrated network of about a dozen regional computer centers using the same basic software. This has greatly enhanced the movement of statistical data from school districts to state government and back. Local districts come and go with regard to participation in the regional centers. Computer sales people like to play the egos of local business administrators, and pretend to demonstrate that local ownership provides economy and control. Many districts have fallen for this line, then have come back pleading for help after botching payrolls and other crucial functions. The obvious solution

154

and the now common practice is to have local hardware tied into the regional network with integrated software.

In returning to BOCES from a fairly prestigious position in a highly regarded University, I enjoyed mixed blessings. On the one hand, I was able to administer in a style somewhat above the dust and smoke of the usual administrative battle ground. On the other hand, I was approaching the modal age for retirement, and was beyond my peak of energy, yet still had to survive all of the perennial challenges of any superintendency.

Having inherited the near-unique situation of zero bonded debt, I was determined to maintain that tradition. We needed additional labs and classrooms, so we designed a cost-effective wing for the Vo-tec Center, and squeezed every possible dollar from the operating budget and convinced the component districts to accept a higher than normal budget for two years in order to avoid bonding. This creative financing required an election, but harking back to the consolidation days, I conducted a blitz of informational meetings and the issue carried by a huge majority.

Later, an auxiliary building was constructed in stages, and entirely by our building trades classes. After the fact, a state official announced that we could not do such a thing. There was a period of blustering and posturing about forfeiture of state funds, but the politicians did not really want to publicly fight fiscal prudence and common sense.

Now that public employee unions were a fact of life, I had some periods of stress involving contract negotiations and grievances. I stayed out of the direct negotiations until that last impasse when the union representatives needed to hear directly from the horse's mouth that every drop of blood had been squeezed from the board; and the board needed to hear directly from me that the union had given every possible inch. These sessions were hard work, but were always successful, hence gratifying. The gut wrenching sessions leading up to this climax always seemed to reach crisis stage while I was traveling. On several trips, I stopped at every rest area to find a pay phone and discuss the

155

latest developments with our chief negotiator. Although I still resist cell phones, they would have been very handy in those days.

1887 Saratoga Swingers - Diamond Jim Brady and Lillian Russell

Grievances usually found their way to me in my role as appeal officer, and I sometimes had to concede that a lower level administrator had goofed. My willingness to admit administrative error was well accepted by both sides, and in a dozen years, I recall only one of my decisions being appealed.

The only union action which I took personally was, in fact, very personal. Each fall, I invited all of the new teachers and the Department chairs to our home for a get-acquainted reception. One year, the contract still had not been settled, but I sent out the usual invitations. This prompted a great debate within the union, and the state AFT office insisted that the local must not participate. On Sunday afternoon, only two chairpersons addressed the mountain of goodies which Peggy had baked, and they were both past presidents of the union. I fully understood the problem of the union, yet at a personal level, I resented the slight to my wife.

CHAPTER THIRTEEN – RETIREMENT AT LAST

Retirement always seemed distant until my younger associates started cashing in at age fifty-five. New York law was changed while I was in higher education, wiping out eligibility for much of my experience in Oregon and Michigan, so I could not think about retirement before my sixties. I watched wistfully as friends started drawing pensions larger than our total family income for most of our lives.

After we finally realized that we could retire if we really desired, job stress dropped sharply, and the last few years passed quickly. At age sixty-three, I rounded off forty years as a public school and private university administrator, which seemed a good time to stop. Two consulting groups invited me to join them, so I polished up my resumes. Very quickly, Ed Dunmire called from western New York and asked if I would consider an interim superintendency. It was close to our grandchildren, so I said, "Sure, I could handle it for a few weeks." When Ed admitted that it could drag on for many months, I declined with thanks and have turned down every such nibble. I did continue for 10 years to teach an alternate year graduate course for the State University of N.Y., for teachers considering school administration. This helped me keep current with the profession, and I was reassured to watch slow but steady improvement in the quality of these potential leaders over the years.

At a dinner in the monumental Hall of Springs with about three hundred family, professional associates and civic leaders (serenaded by opera singers and old friends John Cimino and Diane Legro) our retirement gift was a Love Boat Cruise to Vancouver, B.C., from Anchorage, where late May temperatures were a rare eighty degrees. This incredibly scenic trip gave opportunities to visit old haunts and friends from the 1940's and 50's in Washington and Oregon.

As a student at RPI, Cimino was torn between finishing a technological degree and leaving for a career in music. I counseled him to do both, so after graduating and teaching science for a couple of years, he took his superb natural baritone voice to the Juilliard School. Next, John used every available cent for a ticket to Italy, where he won a major competition opening the door to studying with the top opera coach of the time. During the weeks of study, he lived with the maestro, who refused to take a penny when he realized his usual fee would take all of John's return passage.

John Cimino Impromptu

John won the Pavarotti competition for baritones and appeared on national television with the great tenor. This was followed by many successful engagements and rave reviews in the minor leagues of opera from coast to coast, plus a smash success as a late substitute at the Wexford, Ireland, festival. However, he never made the Met. Instead, he leads a group of similarly talented artists who do wonderful work in the public schools and colleges, inspiring those who hope to make a career of the performing arts, but also using the arts to motivate all levels of students toward better academics and citizenship. This work barely meets expenses, so they help pay the bills by conducting leadership training for corporations. One example was a series of meetings involving all 5000 Starbucks store managers on the theme of leading by serving.

At the retirement dinner, we were surprised to see President Emeritus Dick Folsom and Charles Phelan from California, Sheldon Roberts from Oregon, the Harrods (whom we later drove to Nova Scotia) from Maine, and the Robinsons from Georgia in addition to our family from the Midwest.

Organizer and M.C. Jim Arnold unleashed more fanfare than either of us expected, but it was greatly appreciated.

New York Assemblyman D'Andrea presented a resolution from the legislature, and brother Phil represented the governor of Nebraska in conferring my commission as admiral in the state's Navy.

Brief talks were given by Regent Laura Chodos, Deputy Commissioner Skip Meno, BOCES Chairman Lloyd Brownell, former district superintendent Don Myers, faculty association President, Isaac Labish, and Adirondack Trust President Charles Wait, who succeeded my good friend and tennis partner Pete when he died from smoke inhalation at his Lake George camp. Charles recalled that I had changed the entire direction of the Private Industry Council when I persuaded political and business leaders of the region that we could better serve the goal of job creation and training through a three county organization instead of three separate fiefdoms.

Sheldon, Tom, Betty

Dr. Steve Wiberley did the only real roasting, drawing on the exciting times we shared at RPI.

Briefly into retirement, we realized how little we needed. After feeling limited, though never poor through most of our lives, we now felt truly privileged a half-century from our first real awareness of depression times. However, no amount of money would change significantly the money-stretching habits developed in my early years. Our many wonderful trips still involve careful planning and looking for best buys in transportation, food and lodging. I can now admit my penny pinching proclivities, but I take great joy in the fact that Warren Buffett and several other billionaires share my tightness or good economic sense, depending on your point of view.

A few of my associates complain about boredom in retirement, but I have not had a minute without one project or another demanding attention. Before retiring, I did some scrimshaw and made gold and silver jewelry using nineteenth century dental equipment. In recent years, my craftsmanship (some might call it hammer mechanics) has been directed toward the restoration and repair of antiques.

From the first whalebone cane bought in a Nantucket auction forty years ago, antique collecting was something between an obsession and a disease. We explored countless shops while traveling, and almost learned the full meaning of "buyer beware," especially in auctions which are basically the same whether run by Sotheby's or the local auction barn.

That first cane whetted my interest, not only in walking sticks, but also in scrimshaw and other items made from bone and ivory. It is one of the most durable materials on earth, and lends itself to carving with splendid detail, polish and patina. Some of the oldest museum items are ivory, and while there are many cracks from drying out, curators need not worry about dampness, rust or corrosion.

Canes are as old as recorded history. Starting as clubs for hunting and protection, they quickly became symbols of power, and many societies forbade their possession except by nobility or church leaders. The military version was the swagger stick.

Ownership gradually trickled down through other privileged groups until the "wearing" of a cane was a fashion imperative both for men and women, and the lowest classes finally were allowed to carve and carry a stick from the woods.

Prosperous men and women even changed canes to suit the location and the costume. Few were actually used for support and many had a utilitarian purpose hidden from view (weapons, liquor, illicit drugs, medicines, money, valuables, tools of a trade or profession, cosmetics, alarms, lights, symbols of religion or protest, seats, rods for fishing or locating water, measures for horses, lumber or coffin sizing, etc. etc.)

Part of Cane Collection

Much of the appeal in canes came from the fact that many are damaged and present a restoration challenge. The British brought the finest carved ivory handles from India and the Orient, then proceeded to destroy them by pounding on heavy oak doors (most of which had clearly visible bronze door knockers).

Another appeal was the fact that almost all canes are one-of-a-kind. Our zenith was reached at something over 2000 sticks, with only a handful of duplicates, but we have now reduced to under 1000.

Music boxes also blossomed into a significant collection. Their wonderful craftsmanship, which has allowed them to survive 200 years of usage, is much admired and missed in current society, and causes reproductions to be priced higher than antiques. This eliminates concern for faking, which has taken much of the joy out of certain kinds of antiques such as bronze castings, art glass, scrimshaw and early toys.

Arising from the insatiable demand of post-Renaissance royalty for diversions, music boxes were developed by clockmakers, first as musical timepieces, then as stand-alone instruments capable of magnificent music composed especially for the particular music box, occasion or recipient by such masters as Chopin, Liszt, etc. At one extreme is a movement so tiny that it is hidden in a finger ring, and there also are full orchestras-in-a-box with more than 100 full size instruments. From individual watchmakers, production shifted to cottage industry with each of several families in a village contributing their specialty to the production of a music box. When all phases were combined under one roof, we had the beginning of the Industrial Age, mostly in the French section of Switzerland.

As a collector of both mechanical music and walking sticks, my favorite is a singing bird which pops out of a gold cane handle, sings an authentic bird song while moving its beak, head and wings, then disappears in a flash of tiny feathers. This treasure is safely housed in a private Vienna collection, but probably would bring several million dollars.

In general, we found antique collectors to be pleasant and honest folks, and though perfect strangers, we have been invited into homes

housing extremely valuable collections, sometimes based on nothing but a blind phone call. Through our collector organizations, we have made many long time friends. Conventions always include several open houses to visit the outstanding collections in the area. Until his death, the ultimate host for meetings of the

1860's Box Plays 36 Tunes

Musical Box Society was Murtaugh Guinness, scion of the huge beer and liquor family. He lived in two four story brownstones on East 80th in Manhattan, surrounded by hundreds of music boxes. He looked for the best surviving examples, which were then lovingly restored and serviced by two full-time technicians. Happily, his collection was well endowed and will be displayed by a museum in New Jersey.

Peggy claims that my overzealous collecting, not hers, forced her into the antique business. In any case, we did a number of shows, then went into the Regent Street Antique Center more than 20 years ago. MaryLou Whitney cut the ribbon to open "business" in what had been the original home of Skidmore College. In most winter months, our gross does not even pay the rent, let alone paying someone to cover for us the minimum of one day per week while we are in Florida. However, we have met many interesting people who have heard about our collection, or who simply drop in.

MaryLou Opens

A few of the super-wealthy are hard bargainers (certainly not a crime) and only one ignored letters requesting payment for jewelry somehow overlooked at checkout. Some who come to mind pleasantly include opera greats Beverly Sills and Roberta Peters, Joan Rivers, Sallie Jessie Raphael, Peter Fonda, Jinx Falkenburg, David Cassidy, Ginger Rogers, Mrs. Douglas McArthur and many members of the New York City Ballet and the Philadelphia Orchestra. Most recently, Peggy had a good visit with Peter Martins and Darci Kistler, whose daughter found a treasure. A good customer and lovely lady was Betsy (Mrs. John Hay) Whitney. In her late years, she browsed from a wheelchair admiring and learning provenance, but never asking about price.

Her German house manager would return later and do some serious bargaining. The summer one of Mrs. Whitney's paintings sold for $82,500,000 he was just as serious.

On one occasion, he mentioned that Mrs. Whitney would like a large ivory horsehead cane from the exhibit. When told that, regretfully, it was not for sale, he said, "Oh." The next week, he was back to ask for the price of the horse head, and was told it really was not for sale. Apparently convinced that this was merely a strategy to get top dollar, he kept coming back, finally saying, "you know, Mrs. Whitney really needs this as an important gift for her brother-in-law, Bill Paley (father of CBS). He was speechless when I handed him a huge ivory monogram cane whose swirls spelled "W.P.," but agreed to show it to Mrs. Whitney, who bought it at once.

In a few days, he reappeared, whether on Mrs. Whitney's instructions or his own inability to give up. In any case, he made one last try, leaving us feeling sorry that we could not accommodate such a great lady, yet convinced that a sale would merely confirm the original assumption that everyone has his price.

Other little frustrations and annoyances include those who do not wish to pay sales tax and those who carry dickering too far. Sally Jessie wanted to buy a three dollar item for one dollar and then transport it in her chauffeured Bentley.

Theft is inevitable, but Peggy was specially irked when she was certain that a man had taken the fine carved ivory handle off a cane almost under her nose. She followed him in her car (more bravery than good judgement), but lost him at the track. The police urged her to call them next time.

Most of us have used the term, "idle rich," but the Saratoga summer people maintain a schedule which would kill me. Those who own and/or train horses are up at dawn despite partying virtually every night. Peggy occasionally keeps a sample of invitations we receive to the mostly charitable fund raising events. At several hundred dollars each, we could not begin to attend all of them, though we usually send a token donation except to the many out of town groups who simply try to cash in on the Saratoga ambiance. We keep busy enough by attending ballet, orchestra, chamber music, Skidmore events, and a few more to which we feel personal connections.

JOSEPH BONAPARTE
(miniature on ivory from our collection)

The epitome of the non-idle socialite surely is MaryLou Whitney, who has generously shared her name, time and fortune with Saratoga. For a number of years, we attended her grand balls in the Canfield Casino with its riches of Tiffany stained glass. When racing was extended, the ball conflicted with our family Bash, but we continue to enjoy her hospitality at Cady Hill and the National Museum of Dance (one of the many institutions she has founded and/or nourished). Now happily married to John Hendrickson, she was for decades the

After serving as King of Naples and King of Spain, he came to see Niagara. A weekend in Saratoga turned into so many weeks that brother Napoleon ordered him to return or lose his finances.

faithful wife of Cornelius Vanderbilt Whitney, who founded Pan-American Airlines and Marineland, and financed *Gone with the Wind*. MaryLou returned to serious horse ownership in the past two years, and her relative long shot Birdstone kept Smarty Jones from a near-certain Triple Crown just a year after the local Funnycide suffered the same fate, easily winning the Kentucky Derby and the Preakness, then losing the Belmont.

167

The story of Saratoga's cultural explosion always brings to my mind such disparate names as Whitney, Dake, Mather, Wait, Rockefeller, McKelvie, Ormandy, Balanchine, Hayden, Sills, Houseman, Dutoit, Juillet and dozens of artists who, while not financial movers and shakers, fell in love with the town and shared with us some of their dedication to their respective arts. At the top of this latter group, I would nominate the Alsops. Ruth is principal cellist for the Ballet Orchestra, and Lamar for many years was concert master. In addition to violin and viola, he has mastered saxophone, clarinet and solo whistling. One of our countless memorable Saratoga evenings was his benefit concert for the Luzerne Music Camp at the SPAC little theater. A composer in residence wrote a concerto which featured Lamar with each of his many voices.

The Alsops, like us, had an antique business as an excuse for rampant collecting. They bought the old mansion on Smith Bridge Road (used for filming "Ghost Story," Fred Astaire's last movie) where we enjoyed a number of New Year's parties. Farther back on the property, they have built a new home attached to a large display space for antique cars and other vintage treasures. This has been dubbed "Alsop Hall," the venue for a wonderful series of monthly summer benefits for the Saratoga Council for the Arts, entitled "Chamber Music and All That Jazz." Through their widespread connections in the musical world, they inveigle world class artists to give their services for a weekend in Saratoga. Ruth even plays a major role in preparing the wine and gourmet treats which replace dinner for most of us.

Their daughter, Marin, is the preeminent female conductor, already credited with guest engagements with many of the world's great orchestras.

In gradually lightening up our hoard, we have found much pleasure in giving appropriate items, mostly canes, to about fifteen museums from Jekyll Island, Georgia to Sitka, Alaska. After becoming a collector, I realized that most museum walls were covered with photos and paintings of men and women holding walking sticks, yet the museum might not display a single cane. Few curators have recognized the discrepancy, but most have gratefully accepted offers of a donation. Jekyll Island has restored ten of the mansions which reputedly represented twenty-five percent of the world's total wealth in the late nineteenth century, so we gave them ten sticks, including Tiffany and Gorham examples which undoubtedly were typical for these families.

Golf clearly is a luxury, but since I finally had time to take up the game, I have played more than my share, taking more than my share of strokes. Unlike some married couples we know, Peggy and I really

Timber Pines, Florida

enjoy playing together. Our home on the fairway at Timber Pines makes it possible to go out for a few holes in the evening without pre-planning.

After several vacations in Naples, Florida, we happened to visit Rick and Jane Telander, Peggy's niece, who built in Glen Lakes, north of Tampa, after literally looking the world over for the best escape from the traffic, earthquakes, fires and mud slides of Southern California. Before starting construction, they visited Florida during every month of the year to reassure themselves that the summer heat would be bearable They entertained us in their beautiful home, then directed our attention a few miles south to Timber Pines and the greatest bargain ever for duffers. Three of the four golf courses are free to residents. Three trial rentals, and we were ready to buy a fully furnished home on a fairway. It is a well-kept community with a good cross section of lower middle to upper middle class residents, widely varying facilities and activities, and reasonable taxes.

Though I am not wild about maintaining two houses and lawns, apartments and condos in Saratoga would cost about the same as our very efficient house constructed by Bill Grande forty years ago. It was a National Home manufactured near Frankfort, Indiana.

CHAPTER FOURTEEN – SOME THOUGHTS ON BOARDS; MAKE-YOUR-OWN-SCHOLARSHIP

Educational administrators, of course, are called upon to serve on many civic and charitable boards. I no longer feel guilty in declining such invitations, because most boards repeatedly tap the same narrow pool of talent. This "networking" overlooks huge numbers of intelligent and energetic citizens who have more genuine interest in the various enterprises than do the draftees who serve on more boards than they can juggle. Yes, boards need some experienced members, but there is a distinct advantage in having some innocent beginners to ask questions. Most boards are all too susceptible to rubber stamping the suggestions of administrators and committees – especially those with highly paid executives and large, prestigious organizations. As evidence, I would point to the runaway executive salaries of both corporations and large non-profits, and to the increase in accounting scandals.

Centennial Co-chairs

Some boards I served as member or administrator were delights – well disciplined concerning time management, but always receptive to intelligent questions and devil's advocacy when it appeared that a major position was about to be adopted with little discussion. My worst experiences were with a too large and political church board. When we got around to discussing the wardrobe of the minister's wife, I had had enough. A hospital board also was instructive. Some of the physician members were conscientious and thorough, but others were more obviously interested in protecting staff prerogatives than in improving patient services. As board vice-president, I was given the thankless and difficult challenge of chairing a series of disciplinary hearings when an obstetrician was charged with improper delivery resulting in an infant mortality. Both sides brought in hired gun consultants, one claiming that the procedures had been letter perfect, and the other describing them as criminal.

Philly at Whitney GWTW Ball

A most rewarding assignment in recent years has been as member, then chairman of the selection committee for the Stewart's Scholarship Foundation. With few exceptions,(mainly in treating friends to incredible vacations) our good friend Philly Dake has lived quite modestly despite the legendary success of the ice cream and convenience store chain she helped her husband and then her brother-in-law develop.

One of her creative contributions as executive vice-president was the Make-Your-Own-Sundae, so when she generously funded a scholarship foundation to help dependents of company employees, we started awarding the Make-Your-Own-Scholarship. The message to employees, spouses and children: if you are serious about self improvement through education, financial aid will be found. Many of the counter clerks are modestly paid single mothers, sometimes with two or three children in college, and we have been dumbfounded and delighted by their response in raising the educational goals of their children. Most of the grant recipients have done well and have been most grateful.

Sea Cloud II

During our years at Timber Pines, we have had Philly come for a week between her other winter travels, in a futile effort to match her hospitality. Having had her fill of formal and fancy events the rest of the year, she is the epitome of the low maintenance guest, enjoying wilderness boat rides, mall visits, and just hanging out. We eat simply at home by ourselves or with whatever friends happen to drop in.

Over the years, Philly has entertained us in Saratoga, Hawaii and Bermuda many times. In 2003, she took us on the cruise of a lifetime around Ireland on Sea Cloud II, the 400 foot square-rigged sailing yacht copied after the famous ship owned by Marjorie Meriwether Post. Between sections of the cruise, we put in at the leading castles and gardens for private tours and meals hosted by the surviving nobility of Ireland. Other highlights were the towering abbey of St. Michael's Mount (mirroring Mont Ste. Michele across the English Channel) and the tiny island of Inishmore, so chopped up into home sites and mini-pastures that it reputedly has several thousand miles of stone walls.

Another benefit of the cruise was getting better acquainted with the family of Philly's son, Perrin, wife Estelle and son Grahame (now joined by adoptive sisters from Russia to share their beautiful homes in the Rockies and Friends Lake, N.Y.

Philly was one of the first to cruise on the supership Queen Mary 2, this time taking Peggy, another old friend/neighbor/bridge partner Nancy Downing, and Darla Oathout, a gifted photographer like Philly and soulmate of Bradford Dake. Perhaps even more than others in the family, Brad is fiercely independent, creative and perfectionist. With persistence and with guidance from old school artisans, he has built a castle-like home deep in the Adirondacks. He has become a civic/political force for balanced management of wilderness (impacting even the state constitution) and has earned his page in the folklore of the huge but least populated county of New York.

Before cruising, we participated in dedicating to Philly, a perfect oak tree at Saratoga Performing Arts Center. The tree and its bronze plaque are located so they look out across grass and stonework toward Charlie

Charlie Spring Dedication

Spring honoring her husband. Charlie played a major role in supporting the center, and Philly has been a key member of the board in keeping this marvelous institution strong. The oak tree is only one of many richly deserved recognitions to Mrs. Dake for her community leadership and generosity to hospitals, colleges, cultural organizations, etc.

174

CHAPTER FIFTEEN – OTHER TRAVEL

As suggested above, our married life started with a flurry of travel, including the super-extended trip back to OSC from Indiana. In all of our years in Oregon, virtually every year provided some excuse to visit Indiana, and we took great pains to avoid duplicating our routes. After five years of marriage, we had touched all forty-eight of the states existing at that time, though it took a few years to add Hawaii and Alaska.

A single volume could not report all of the exciting destinations and the experiences in reaching them. Most trips were rushed because of my professional commitments, but after retirement, we were able to schedule a leisurely train trip through Italy, Switzerland, France, the Netherlands, Belgium, and England. After fending off the gypsy pickpockets in Rome (one reached inside my shirt going after the body pouch), we had a thoroughly pleasant journey.

We had corresponded with a psychiatrist cane collector in Siena who hosted us for several days in a spacious apartment covering the ground floor of their three story stone home overlooking the city. I do not recall the age of the building, but a carving over the entrance commemorates a historic visit by Garibaldi. There still are differences in our cultures, because this obviously upscale home had laundry lines running from windows to poles in the back lawn. Also, when they later visited our home, they were fascinated by our garbage disposal unit.

Dr. Traballesi collected only those canes carved as owls, the symbol of the pie-slice section of Siena where he was raised and later became the elected leader. The seventeen sub-cities, or contrade, sponsor entries in the Palio, the wildest horse race in the world, dating back 1000 years. The town square slopes considerably and is paved with stone worn smooth by centuries of use. The race course consists of three tight curves and a right angle turn just before the horses slide into the 200 foot tower. Race sponsors continue the honored tradition of kidding themselves by sprinkling soil on the track, but it still serves better as a skating rink.

Preparation for the race never stops, and winning is all-important. We saw movies of a race where the jockey who barely missed victory was attacked by citizens of arguably one of the (otherwise) most civilized cities in the world.

Each contrada has a community building which is a combination museum and Civic Center, also serving to distribute charity. Our host had induced a lady to leave her estate to build a fine new community center. Although he is a lovable man and had been highly respected, he was voted out of office. His detractors pointed out that he had missed their one opportunity to bribe every jockey in the race.

Siena is delightfully unspoiled. The garish neon signs which we take for granted are permitted only at the hotels on the access road

Palio From Tower

outside the Old City, and passenger cars are not allowed inside the gates except for special cases like doctors. The City tower includes a museum with walls covered floor to ceiling by old masters, yet the windows are open to birds and violent changes of humidity.

The Traballesis went to great trouble to gain access to the non-tourist gems, including a monastery seriously damaged by U.S.

176

bombers in 1943. Our guide pulled many treasures out of drawers, and he assured us that they harbor no ill feelings because they are next to a strategic rail line which surely needed to be taken from fascist control. Besides, the Americans later returned the missing center piece from a Della Robbia masterpiece.

Although we did provide advice and entertainment to our friends when they later came to N.Y., we could not equal their hospitality.

San Gimigniano Towers

Fearing that they would not have another chance, they insisted on covering our entire country in one trip.

Other highlights of that trip to Europe included our stay in Lucerne, Switzerland, and our visit to the National Museum of Street Organs and Mechanical Music in Utrecht, The Netherlands. The director belongs to our society, speaks perfect English, and gave us a personal tour of their collection which logically includes the finest Dutch musical clocks of the kind which gave us so much pain.

London is the city which we have enjoyed visiting the most, even though nine days of a twelve- day visit were spent at Heathrow Airport, probably a record. My first serious sciatic attack germinated during the flight from New York, yet I insisted on doing one of the major antique flea markets. Our hotel was incorrectly booked for only one night instead of five; London was jammed with tourists taking advantage of a favorable exchange rate, so we had no choice but to return to a hotel at Heathrow. Management provided a wheelchair and introduced me to socialized medicine by calling a doctor to the room. He was competent and friendly, and apologized for the required twenty dollar charge to non-citizens.

Hotel staff went out of their way to be helpful. They explained that guests normally stayed for a single night, and they also may have felt some responsibility when Peggy twisted an ankle while pushing my wheelchair to the restaurant. She survived by leaning on the chair, but it required great effort

Big Ben from Big Wheel

on her part. When we recovered enough to visit Oxford, she discovered that the difficult pushing was caused by two flat tires, not the hotel carpeting we had blamed.

Peggy traded the stick-shift rental car for an automatic transmission and proceeded with our planned trip through Wales even though she previously had left the wrong way driving to me. We succeeded in finding the two known ancestral Evans locations, but one was no more than a crossroads requiring us to open and close several gates keeping the multitudinous sheep in their proper pastures. I appreciated Peggy's extra effort in finally getting us to the beautiful and peaceful land of my forebears.

For many years, we were guests of RPI trustee Phil Grove at his home on Harbour Island, and he encouraged us to suggest other guests whom we would enjoy. Financially, it was no bargain, because you almost could not get there from here, but these were the most restorative vacations we ever experienced. Around 1965, the route was through Miami to Nassau to North Eleuthera, then by boat to the island. However, we also bypassed the little boat by using a seaplane, and twice took a short-takeoff-landing plane to the Harbor Island airport. In the short life of this strip, numerous wrecks lined the runway and every one remained at the time of our last visit. The problem was that the single strip was oriented with the narrow dimension of the island, and the prevailing condition was a ninety degree crosswind. Also, there was no money for excavation. The strip merely followed the contour of the ridge so that we landed on a sharp up slope, and before we could apply brakes, we were on the down slope. The boat definitely was the better solution.

The main activity both for natives and visitors was relaxation. Mr. Grove had an arrangement with the Pink Sands resort, named for the beautiful pink beaches, for his guests to use the tennis courts, and I

Ancestral Wales

usually jogged down the trail looking for a game while others napped. The resort was well known in tennis circles, so I usually connected. My best match was with Mike Wallace of Sixty Minutes. We each had a set when it was a time for his boat to leave.

Occasionally, a strong wind would be blowing the length of the tennis court, and I could pull out all the stops with my infamous lob game. I drove both friends and foes to distraction by hitting lobs so high that the enemy would lose all composure before the ball returned to earth. The strong and steady ocean breeze made it possible to hit the ball far beyond the court and have it return from behind my opponents.

My earliest recollection of travel was the Evans family camping trip. Mother had decided that the depression notwithstanding, her sons must see the nation's capitol. We saw the sights of Washington, Atlantic City, etc., and mother told me that the total cost was thirty-eight dollars. Of course, she spent more time cooking, washing dishes and juggling clothing for three boys than she did sightseeing, but was always grateful that her family could share such an experience.

CHAPTER SIXTEEN – NO LONGER UNMENTIONABLE

Since I no longer worry about personal views interfering with organizational missions, I can mention the unmentionables – politics and religion, medical care, even sex.

Truly independent of party politics, my first registration was Republican, for Eisenhower, and I have left it unchanged despite regular ticket splitting as a social liberal and a fiscal conservative. Bush is likeable and I am not thrilled with Kerry, but I feel little in common with the Rove/Cheney group who pretended to unify the nation through compassionate conservatism.

From the first days in office, they mocked that promise by abrogating treaties without consulting Congress, slowing stem cell research which could solve many remaining medical dead-ends, plunging the national treasury into record deficits, making appointments mostly guaranteed to polarize rather than unify, and swaggering up to world problems with an arrogance which has left us virtually alone to defend against exploding numbers of terrorists.

Apologies to my friends who are sincerely loyal to the fading memory of Lincoln's party, but it cannot retain the support of centrist voters while pandering to extremists.

Until disabled by his character flaws, Bill Clinton unified a strong majority of Americans by disavowing the extremists of his party, reforming welfare, and balancing budgets.

If either party could produce candidates willing to follow Clinton's lead without the sexual distractions, that party could control Washington for a long time. On the other hand, I have been happiest when the President's party did not control both houses of Congress. Those have been the periods when we truly validated our system of checks and balances. Legislative and administrative abuses were more likely to surface, and Presidents were forced to nominate centrists rather than extremists.

Having offended loyalists of both parties, I will proceed to shock and outrage true believers of all the great world religions.

Although I belong to the United Methodist Church and consider myself religious, I would not be welcome on the rolls of the typical church which charts in great detail the only road map to heaven.

There is beautiful truth in the writing and teaching of all the great religions, and virtually no contradiction in their various descriptions of the good life leading to heaven. Therefore, I see no point in proselytizing the faithful of any religion, and I would confine missionary work to (1) the multitudes who have no compass and are desperately seeking direction; (2) the disadvantaged through self-help projects like Habitat and Heifer; and (3) the dispossessed, to the extent that we find the necessary Mother Theresas to heal and nourish them.

Getting into heaven does not worry me, because I was born into heaven. On darker days, when I can find nothing good in the world, it is because I am looking in the wrong places.

The hereafter does not frighten me, because whatever survives of my spirit will be inseparable from the universal spirit of good humans, good thoughts, good deeds.

While respecting and learning from the Bible and other great religious works, I found my personal direction summed up in the brief replies of two non-theologians who were asked about their beliefs.

Medical missionary Dr. Albert Schweitzer, "Reverence for Life."

Architect Frank Lloyd Wright, "What we can know of God, we may learn from the body of God, which we call Nature."

The orthodoxy of almost any church must label me "godless," because as much as I was impressed by the Sistine Chapel, my God is not an old man with a beard. Rather, she is an ageless Mother Earth, if you will, yet encompassing countless macro and micro stages beyond our vision, reach or comprehension. Life is that "beautiful mystery."

Jesus and other prophets are gods to me, because the highest purpose of organized religion should be to lead the evolution of a more perfect lifestyle, not just amnesty for the past and insurance for the future. Jesus certainly taught and lived that lifestyle to a unique and superhuman degree, regardless of whether some of his teachings were illustrative parables or literal prescriptions, natural or supernatural.

Another Robert Greenleaf essay defined the optimum lifestyle as comprising beauty, momentaneity, openness, humor and tolerance. These categories concentrate on "being," and while Jesus probably would not quibble with them, he certainly was more concerned with "doing" – explicit charity and ministry.

In this much less than articulate confession, my purpose is not to shake the faith of any believer, because I want to live in a world filled with people who believe in something. As a student, I was shocked and turned off by the hypocritical machinations and excesses of priests, prelates and politicians who used them. With time, I have realized that religion also has inspired superhuman accomplishments in music, art, architecture, literature and service to humanity. I am simply describing my own belief that humans can only speculate about our creation. It is possible that the universe may indeed be timeless, may always have existed through reincarnations of the eternal energy forms. Berlinski's doctrine of intelligent uncertainty angered both atheists and fundamentalists, so it can't be all bad.

Above all, spare me from the zealots who not only have all the answers, but also are determined to impose them on the world. If possible, keep them from holding guns or public office, because they have crucified saints and prophets, fueled the inquisitions, triggered most wars, and blocked the progress of science and medicine.

Each religion describes miracles proving its exclusive route to heaven, but what miracle could surpass the simplicity of a sunset or the complexity of life systems in even "lower forms of life?" Millions, from theologians to believers to zealots, would complain that my version of God shows a beautiful but empty landscape. I would expand Frank Lloyd Wright's little definition ever so slightly by adding, "and human nature."

While not as Godlike as we pretend in both politics and religion, humans do represent the "highest" product of evolution TO DATE, perhaps demonstrating both the godliness of evolution and the evolution of godliness. The observation and contemplation of human nature (best and most efficiently summarized by the few years of Jesus' teachings) have validated the characteristics of Godlike living and the higher mental/moral sensitivities which have evolved in man. Some of these "higher instincts" certainly are learned or reinforced by learning, but I would like to believe that even a child raised in a social vacuum might possess some trace of empathy and compassion. Something long ago passed along to Philo of Alexandria the sensitive conviction, "Be kind– everyone you meet is waging a great battle."

To date, no civilized government excepting Oregon has followed the lead of the Dutch in legalizing euthanasia, but I am confident that this melding of American traditions (fiscal responsibility, democracy, freedom to buy preferential treatment, government sponsored gambling, and avoidance of hard decisions) will be enthusiastically adopted by both Houses when I become President.

Politicians talk much and do little about the worsening financial crisis of Medicare and Social Security. Despite losing some doctors to exorbitant insurance costs and excessive paper work, our medical machinery works amazingly well.

The budget must be balanced, and a logical place to start is a serious war on fraud, but most older Americans also know that we are trying too hard to extend life by over-treating our medical ills. Most of us have received numerous therapy sessions which could have been self directed after minimal instruction. Granted that many of us are less likely to carry through without hand holding, the separation of the motivated from the unmotivated might somewhat ameliorate the problem of living too long.

Every few months, we read that some misguided or deranged nurse has been arrested for hastening the demise of too many nursing home patients. This can not be tolerated, of course, and I should not speak about it so flippantly, but any extended visit to a nursing home makes one wonder how much of a favor we are doing some of the longer residents.

184

When Dr. Joe Pahl passed away recently, he gained his relief only because he was lucid and forceful enough to order the cessation of endless procedures. He told me that as a physician, he felt some responsibility to serve as a guinea pig to train young doctors, but only up to a point.

No one wants a patient to die on his shift, so nursing homes send their critical patients back to hospitals and hospitals attach wires and tubes despite living wills. Are you ready for the solution? Follow the lead of Oregon and the Netherlands and make euthanasia legal. Indeed, go further and make euthanasia easily and inexpensively available. If you really believe in "Choice," at least for adults, help those who are suffering and see no future by giving them a pill which allows them to die painlessly at a time of their choosing. This is morally right, at least according to my definition of morality, because no one should be condemned to suffer needlessly and involuntarily. And it has the side benefit for the rest of society that it would markedly reduce the cost of medical care.

Euthanasia by choice would be far better than another proposal: When all lesser efforts to balance the budget have failed and we have discovered how to report the national deficit when "trillions" becomes inadequate, we can turn to our favorite indoor sport – the government sponsored lottery. After age seventy, each year of longevity would increase the odds that a medicare drug prescription would include a euthanasia pill terminating medicare membership. Heavier weighting could be assigned for people with very expensive illnesses.

Throughout recorded history, people of means have been able to buy what they hope will be extended life, so the lottery will allow individuals to pay highly progressive premiums for reduced odds, but our democratic principles require that no one should be allowed to completely buy his way out.

In the final stage of the game, players would be allowed to reverse options and pay progressive means-based premiums to increase the odds of receiving the silver bullet and bring an end to suffering. This melding of American traditions (fiscal responsibility, democracy, freedom to buy preferential treatment, AND government sponsored gambling) should please almost everyone.

(Now I will follow Peggy's orders and confess that some of the ranting on medical care was tongue-in-cheek).

The first hours of 2003 reminded me that in my second childhood, I should not repeat the string of accidents and near misses in my early years. I spent four hours, soaking wet, in an emergency room wheelchair, waiting for staff to locate an orthopedic surgeon so he could confirm that some pain killer would not interfere with his re-setting of my dislocated shoulder (both shoulders also were broken, which the doctor had never seen before). The low point came when a nurse told me to stop my violent shaking from cold and pain.

Four hours after one small glass of wine, I had gone out into a heavy rain and tripped over the grey concrete parking barrier extending partly across the end of the sidewalk where we were visiting, then executed a swan dive onto the pavement.

In addition to wiping out my right rotator cuff, the shock of the accident sent my heart out of the sinus rhythm which had only recently been restored by electrical cardioversion in a brief hospital stay (the doctors this time decided to leave it out of rhythm; I am living very nicely with atrial fibrillation).

Just as my shoulders were healing, I learned about wheelchairs and walkers when my back misbehaved at the Bash in Austin. Fortunately, I had an early warning signal and was able to get last minute plane reservations instead of driving.

In treatment for shoulders and back, I spent much time in medical anterooms filling out forms and listing previous problems. It was impressive to catalog from modern times: toenail fungus, herniated discs causing both right and left sciatic distress, numbness of both legs, hernia repair, prostate biopsy, thyroid nodule, colon polyps, squamous cell carcinomas on neck, finger and ear, precancerous zaps by the dozen, silent heart attack, arrythmia, fibrillation, cataracts, glaucoma, fractured shoulders, severed biceps, wiped out rotator cuff and second-time root canals. All this in a guy with good health! Perhaps our health care

186

system is doing a pretty good job in keeping me physically active, feeling well and with bodily functions at least resembling those of my youth.

As newlyweds, we decided that our real honeymoon (not the hurried weekend pass) should end on our 71st anniversary, with a game of tennis, or perhaps golf, my 90th birthday cake, good wine, lovemaking with classical music and peaceful sleep. Scarcely an anniversary has passed without one of us reminding the other of this promise.

Frequently, this discussion has ended with Peggy asking if I thought I could stand to make love to a woman of fifty (sixty, seventy, eighty). Believe me, it has been easy at every stage. Lovemaking depends on the heart, memory, anticipation and imagination, not athleticism, reason, routine or good vision. At every date, less frequent to be sure, I remember (therefore, I find) Peggy as the beautiful young woman I was blessed to marry and who has become only better and more precious over time.

While enjoying our lives in N.Y. and Florida, we realize that our independence will not last forever. After visiting retirement homes with nursing facilities in Frankfort (where Jane and both of our own mothers have lived), Chapel Hill (where Allen and Margaret have moved), and Hanover (near Eric and Anne), we made a deposit at Woodlawn, which would "guarantee" our admission to Wesley Manor in Saratoga. They will allow us to pass over a couple of openings without prejudice and would welcome my service as resident technician for the reproducing grand piano we donated. Also, it would be a move of just over one mile from Salem Drive .

I confess that retirement homes would be much more attractive if there were not so many old people around, but I recall that when Mother was considering the move, we all reflected on how much Wesley needed her, musically and otherwise. She went in a spirit of service, and she made Wesley a better and more pleasant place for residents and staff as well as herself.

Rupert and Mary K are doing the same thing in Urbana, conducting current events updates, facilitating discussion groups, arranging concerts and lectures, improving shop and computer rooms and equipment, and regularly needling management to consult and involve residents as intelligent adults with a shared mission.

When Jane returns to Frankfort from Florida each year, that Wesley Manor becomes more lively, and Peggy always has had a similar effect on her various communities. Whatever our age when we make the move, we are determined to lower the effective age of the residents.

Montage by Lisa

CHAPTER SEVENTEEN – OUR GROWING FAMILY TREE

Grandkids

Like most whose clock is running down, my chief regret is that I did not take more time with family, and did not give them more help along the way. My exaggerated view of personal/professional ethics (self righteousness) insisted that they be treated exactly like anyone else, and especially in the school systems I administered. Ethics were very important to me, and still are, yet the process of writing these pages revealed to me that my record was not Simon pure. Fortunately, all of our children and grandchildren turned out extremely well in spite of what I did or did not do. Peggy, of course, was a wonderful mother and model.

Eric Alan Evans, our oldest son, always appeared to have an easy road in academics, athletics and socializing. At times, he appeared to set his sights a trifle low to make certain that he would not experience rejection. Several outstanding teachers and counselors made themselves heard at the right time to adjust his aim, e.g. the counselor who insisted that he should apply to the University of Pennsylvania. When his acceptance package arrived, he quickly decided that although he had been captain of an undefeated basketball team, he would never make it in Ivy League competition. After reading about all of the other available sports, he announced that he would make the rugby team. Peggy and I laughed, not taking him seriously because a childhood kidney disease ruled out football. Rugby is an insane version of football, but without the protective gear. So he ended up as captain of the rugby team both in college and law school, with nothing worse than a fractured ankle and a broken tooth.

As president of his fraternity at the time of a disastrous, but not fatal, fire, he received experience far beyond that of most students. Like many fraternities, his had southern roots, and the University would not approve the rebuilding of the house unless the national fraternity updated its traditionally exclusionary membership language. Eric found himself in a squeeze which required patience, tact and mediation at a level which later served him well as an attorney specializing in labor and contract problems.

The countless hours spent in fraternity business and social affairs were not reflected in his transcript, but a strong aptitude test and interview gained admission to the Albany Law College of Union University. However, a very low draft number required him first to meet his military obligation on active duty in the National Guard unit in Saratoga Springs. While waiting to start law school, he had the extraordinary good fortune to share a house with his boyhood buddy, Chaz Dake. Through him, Eric met Anne Van Vechten Myers, a Skidmore senior who became his wife. Eric continued a close relationship with Chaz until his tragic death in a quarry accident.

Anne's father, Dr. Warren Powers Laird Myers, commuted from Rye to his work as Vice-President of Sloan Kettering Memorial Hospital. His weekend relief was working on a retirement home in the Vermont foothills across the river from Dartmouth College, which may help explain why Eric's family all love that area.

Just as Peggy had done for me, Anne practiced nursing to supplement Eric's student loans. They never asked us for help, and received only care packages and one sizeable dental job. This self reliance was reflected in Eric's law school record, which earned him membership in the prestigious Justinian Society.

Anne decided that she would earn a master's degree as a nurse practitioner, applying only to the University of Rochester. Eric matched her optimism by applying only at Harter, Secrest in Rochester. They were the Avis (100 lawyers) to the Hertz of Rochester – Nixon, Peabody (570 lawyers). Both Anne and Eric had highly successful and satisfying careers, though Anne had some interruptions for motherhood. Despite these, Anne became an acknowledged expert on diabetes.

Eric terrified all of us by having a slight stroke at age thirty-four. Thankfully, there has been no further problem, and doctors speculated that he may have been born with undersized arteries to the brain, and that the body may have compensated by developing alternative vessels. In spite of this or because of it (?) they made an early decision that he would retire at age fifty-five. At age fifty-two, he was made the managing partner of the firm despite announcing his resolve to serve for only three years. During his tenure, he had the great satisfaction of having *The Corporate Board Member* magazine directors' survey rank the firm above Nixon for the first time ever. This was reaffirmed in his final year, and he presided over the firm's move to the elegant Bausch and Lomb Building, literally looking down on their friendly rivals at Nixon.

The new home of Eric and Anne is in Hanover, New Hampshire, where Anne is a faculty member in hepatology research at Dartmouth Hospital. Eric is examining his second career options and has been admitted to the bar in that area.

Anne is a splendid mother, but only after great difficulty in childbirth. Both Kathy and Peggy spent many weeks in the household while Anne was confined to bed. The first birth, of Ryan Van Vechten Evans came after only seven months, and was a near miracle. After being on pure oxygen to survive, we were warned that he might expect significant damage to his eyes or brain. During the days of uncertainty, we were encouraged to hold and speak to him. I did this very gingerly, but Dr. Myers handled Ryan with all of the love, skill and dedication of a grandfather-physician. During the long hours of waiting for the alternating signals, good and bad, he wrote of his thoughts in a premature nursery (excerpted):

The ultimate beauty: A mother's look.
The ultimate tenderness: Her touch
On her infant's cheek.
He knows her touch and her voice and
Knowing, he opens his eyes,

Ryan and Tina

He stretches; he tries out
The wonders of arms, hands, legs, and feet.
At seven months?
How can it be?
After all the warnings about possible severe disability, we did not know whether to pray for survival or for deliverance from a potentially tragic semi-existence. Ryan now is serving his residency in neurology in that very hospital. This was his first choice and it facilitates owning a house midway between his work and that of Tina, a primary school teacher. Both his grandfathers probably would have opted for the prestige of Harvard/Mass General, but that certainly was not the path I followed personally.

Ryan has been both talented and fortunate in his academic choices. In high school, his priorities led to national ranking as a squash player, so he was not at the very top of his class. However, he applied only to Dartmouth, where he had many pleasant memories of childhood experiences with the Myers,' and his squash credentials plus good board scores and interview gained his acceptance. In similar fashion, he was accepted to tough Columbia Medical College and graduated with high honors, entering the profession he had always wanted. Not only following the professional lead of his grandfather, Dr. W.P.L. Myers, Ryan also has inherited or emulated his gentle disposition and caring dedication.

Katharine Gray Evans has the same sunny disposition as her older brother, and perhaps even more determination. Now finishing veterinary medicine at Cornell University, she was a fine high school athlete, leading in field hockey and skiing. Cornell does not have varsity skiing, but as an undergraduate, she was captain of the club team.

Since her early childhood, Katie has wanted only to treat animals, so it is fortunate that her hard work and persistence have gained admission to this highly competitive field. Her love of life, both human and animal, shines through, and she will surely be a great success as a professional and as a mother. As of this writing, she has announced her

Cornell Grad Katie

engagement to Andy, a professional engineer, and they plan to live in the Vermont mountains.

Irrepressible Andrew, youngest of the family, is beginning his senior year at the University of Vermont with emphasis in ornamental horticulture. Blessed with a sunny disposition and natural athletic talent, like the others, Drew has been a good student. In addition to his outstanding skiing and percussion work, he has found time to become proficient on more kinds of bicycles than I knew existed, and he has shown staying power in part time and vacation jobs in bicycle repair, gardening and garden sales.

Our younger son, Philip Irwin Evans, probably is the most broadly knowledgeable of any member of the family. Like his brother, he is extremely sensitive to the feelings of others and is an outstanding natural athlete. While growing up, he would never accept the fact that he was younger than Eric and his friends, and through sheer determination, he

Anne With High School Graduate Andrew

frequently matched their skill levels. During his eleventh grade, they had the great fun of playing together on an undefeated basketball team (until post season when they were totally psyched out in the home gym of Troy High School).

As graduation approached, Phil had strong college boards, but did not show great interest in any of the colleges we visited. This was not really surprising, because he was not demonstrative in nature. I tried to be subtle in my pressing, but managed to leave St. Lawrence University literature strewn all across his path, and he selected it, probably more to please me than to demonstrate genuine conviction. It had seemed to offer a great blend of academic standing, manageable size and opportunity to continue into college the basketball he seemed to enjoy so much. Although he was doing acceptable academic work and

194

appeared to be ahead of schedule in basketball, he simply was not a happy camper.

After leaving S.L.U., Phil met his future wife by way of his best friend, Dan Harris. Lisa Marie Milanese, daughter of Lucy and John Milanese, RPI alumnus and prominent Capital District realtor, was the younger sister of Julie, Dan's future wife.

Phil and Lisa went to Boston, where he studied geology and she specialized in early childhood education at Wheelock college. Phil eventually went into computer operation and programming,

Alison's High School Graduation

where he did quite well without the college degree. However, we were extremely proud of him for completing a degree, with honors, at Siena College a few years ago.

In searching for themselves, Phil and Lisa gave invaluable support to each other.

Siena Grad Phil, with Ali and Lisa

Much later, we learned from Allen's daughter, Mary Margaret, that they also helped her greatly when she was adjusting to her college experience at Katharine Gibbs. After Lisa graduated from Wheelock College, she obtained a primary

school teaching position in Greenville, South Carolina. Phil found a computer position nearby, and they soon married. Lisa was extremely successful and happy as a teacher, but when they were

Ali's Great-grandmothers, Ford and Evans

expecting a child, they quickly decided that the New York schools were more promising. Metropolitan Life did not want to lose Phil, so he was offered a choice of the two New York State locations — Manhattan and Long Island. Long Island seemed the lesser of evils, but a few weeks of traffic gridlock away from Lisa were enough to prompt a gutsy decision: with a pregnant wife, he resigned his job and they bought a townhouse in Clifton Park, N.Y., then began serious job hunting in the Capitol district. Before long, he landed a position with Blue Cross, where he progressed until they outsourced his department with IBM. Big Blue put him on their payroll and left him physically where he had been, with one important difference. While continuing to serve Empire Blue Cross, his team now has some twenty additional corporate clients to keep happy.

Too wise to continue basketball into middle age, Phil discovered another way to punish knees – the game of squash, and has become quite good. Lisa is a talented artist and gardener, and has taken over much of the management of her father's business.

Since Phil and Lisa live only twenty miles from Saratoga, they have taken on the responsibility to look after our affairs while we are in Florida, and this has been much appreciated. They have made many trips to make certain the house is secure, and have met many flights for both sets of parents.

A few years back, I made what I expected to be a donation to a charity, and learned that I was the lucky winner of a Super Bowl package for two in Phoenix. My first day inclination was to decline the prize, but Phil suggested that I avoid any hasty decision. He and I ended up using the tickets, and it was indeed an experience, though once is enough. My resolve was tested a second time as we were flying into Phoenix. A flight hostess announced that the passenger in 17 B desperately needed some tickets to the game and would pay at least $1,600 for a pair. Our seats were clearly better than average, so who knows what he might have paid. However, we were glad to

Milanese Grandparents

see the game with all of its excesses inside and outside the stadium, watch one of O.J. Simpson's lawyers grandstand in the parking lot, play golf at one of the pricey clubs and climb Camelback Mountain. All of the experiences were priceless except the climb, where I made the mistake of trying to keep up with Phil, soon finding myself totally winded for the first time. Later, I learned that I probably had a silent heart attack.

My hazy recollection is that the Dallas Cowboys won over the Pittsburgh Steelers, but the football game ranks very low in the lasting impressions of my best visit with Phil.

The baby which brought them back to New York turned out to be Alison Amy Evans, our fourth brilliant and beautiful grandchild. She won many honors in high school, and is now in her senior year at Colgate University, spending a portion of the year studying in Manchester, England. Ali is very much oriented toward helping people, and is considering a career teaching and/or counseling children confined to hospitals for an extended period.

Quality of public and private education varies greatly across the country, but is much better than politicians would have us believe. The loudest critics have failed miserably in providing financial support needed to bring up quality, and the vast majority of teachers deliver far more than they receive. Our children and grandchildren have received excellent education, though admittedly in two of the better school districts in a better than average state.

During my seventy-plus years attending, administering and observing schools, I have heard the same complaints and have seen the public, school boards and university professors rediscover phonics, holistic reading, old math, new math, etc., over and over. With any one method or approach, the best of teachers will be frustrated by a certain proportion of non-learners. The simple fact is that we all learn at different rates and with different mixes of oral, aural and hands-on experiences. If we insist on putting twenty to thirty students in a class, then we must offer all of the methods to that class. To really improve our teaching-learning performance, we should take the time to look at each child as an individual, determine the most efficient learning methods for that individual, and then utilize the best brains and technologies to deliver to each student the right method for the occasion.

When our nation commits itself to solving a major problem of war, space exploration or public health, we dedicate significant funding to research the problem, develop prototype alternative solutions, and then disseminate one or more of the most promising solutions. This has never been done with education, and a few billion dollars thoughtfully spent could produce huge and continuing improvements in both public and private systems. Incidentally, my years in trying to bring the best and brightest students to RPI convinced me that with the exception of a few inner cities, private education has no advantage whatsoever over the public schools.

Our grand children are just beginning to marry, so we have no great grand children to report as yet. However, our in-laws, nieces and nephews have led interesting and productive lives which must be acknowledged in tribute to the expertise and passion for genealogy possessed by Rupert's first wife, Barbara Jean Barbre Evans.

Although a foundling with almost no clues to her own roots, Jean delighted in helping others trace their families, beginning with the Evans tribe. While traveling with Rupert on his research and consulting assignments, she may have visited more genealogical libraries and sources than anyone before or since, and she taught and wrote on the subject.

After Jean passed away suddenly and peacefully, her daughters, without hesitation, gave their blessing to the marriage of Rupert to their "other mother" of a half-century, Mary Kay Farber, who had been a neighbor and executive assistant in the University of Illinois College of Education. They now are residents and shaker-movers of a fine retirement complex virtually surrounded by the University.

Rupert's firstborn, Ellen, married Roger Collins, a chemical warfare officer who flew many helicopter missions in Vietnam. They own a large stationery and framing business in Hagerstown, Md., and with Alice and Maureen raised, they train guide dogs for the blind. Alice is Mrs. Michael Poel, with son Christian. Maureen married Douglas Margevich and they have daughters Loran and Susan.

Catherine married Ronald Westman, also a career Army officer, and as foster parents of last resort they have salvaged a number of children with incredible physical and emotional challenges, adopting all they could possibly afford (some have astronomical medical expenses). Thus far, Christopher, Alyssa and Shante have joined the original sons, Daniel (wife Alexandra) and Michael (married to Tina) in suburban Omaha.

Nancy picked up Hazel's torch as organist and music teacher. Married to Paul McNabb, founder of a software security company, they have sons Evan, Andrew, Peter and Stewart.

Brother Allen went to war from Frankfort, but returned to our parents' home in Boonville, Indiana, where he fell in love with a sports writer, Margaret Spradley. They recently moved to a retirement community near their children in North Carolina.

Their first daughter, Allene, has had an exciting career in law, making the London Times as the "honey blonde Texan" who had defeated the unbeatable Lloyd's of London. She married Tom Herod, documentary film producer in Austin, Texas, and they co-produced a very expensive daughter, Elizabeth, well beyond the normal child-bearing age for Allene.

Mary Margaret and her husband, Gary both were in hotel management. She now works for a large California travel broker who thought enough of her work to insist that she continue even after moving to Raleigh, North Carolina. When Cuba began opening up to tourism from Canada and Europe, Mary Margaret arranged a reception where Fidel Castro was to give a brief welcome. He was so impressed that he invited himself to stay for dinner.

Tall Tom is a bluegrass musician and wood products executive in North Carolina. Although he has not fathered children, he loves them, and in addition to adopting Cory and Shana, he is raising Cory No. 2 with his present wife, Terri.

Allen's youngest, Beth is a very busy interior designer and mother of Jenkyn, Clinton, Evan, and Karyn with husband Richard Kittrell, an engineer in the Baltimore area. The boys have excelled in acrobatic gymnastics, and Evan has won major dance competitions, incredibly performing a partner lift at the age of ten.

Brother Phil married Elmabeth Hemenway, a Boonville schoolmate and music teacher/real estate broker.

Phil and Beth's son Douglas is a lawyer and law librarian in New Orleans, married to Lisa MauffrayEvans, a career Navy officer and lawyer. Their children are Louis and Katherine.

Since Phil passed away, daughter Jane Evans Burns and children Jennifer and Kevin have lived with Beth in her suburban Omaha home. Jane resumed and completed her undergraduate study with honors, and is now in a doctoral program, commuting to Lincoln.

Switching to Peggy's family, her oldest sister was Roberta Irwin, Ph.D., who passed away after a long career with the National Security Agency, where she was awarded the highest honor given for civilian service to government.

Peg's Sisters at Lake George

Julia, a retired teacher, is married to Ted Fairburn, whose rich bass voice and interest in electronics made him a natural for a career in radio announcing. They have kept their home in Rockford, Ill., but enjoy renting near us in Florida each winter.

Daughter Cynthia recently lost a long and brave struggle with cancer, leaving husband and retired colonel John Thurlow and daughters Irja Bonafede and Julie.

Anne is married to Dr. Gary Olsen, a dentist in Aledo, Illinois, and serves as office manager. Their daughters are Heather (married to John Schlicting) and Marcella (husband Matthew Phillips).

Julia's youngest is Nancy, wife of Chris Olson, a manager with QuadGraphics, printing major magazines. Their sons are Frank and Kenneth.

Jane Irwin Rodgers lost husband Ed, a Chrysler executive, far too soon. She is barely retired from advertising and real estate, but now enjoys living with us seasonally in Florida.

Her oldest, Janey Telander, lives with husband Rick in another golf community just a few miles north of our Timber Pines. They continue to keep us and our house out of trouble, especially in the six months we spend in Saratoga.

Second daughter Susan Robey teaches near Frankfort, and husband Scott works in advertising and consulting. Their children are Sarah and Bradley.

Numbers three and four are twins. I can differentiate now, but for years they were both Barberly.

Barbara Johnson is a nursing administrator married to Ted, the most highly regarded attorney in Frankfort. Their children are Ross, Amanda, and Neil.

Beverly Holloway is a teacher in Virginia Beach. Husband Jim retired after serving as commander of the Atlantic squadron (half of our submarine fleet) and is now a Raytheon executive with projects ranging from Guam to the Amazon to Antarctica. Their daughters are Cheryl Holloway Tutwiler (who just gave birth to daughter Erin) and Gayle Holloway Marsh.

We have lost touch with the Evans cousins (Uncle Bob's large family), but the Bash has kept us close to the Rupert-Jones line. Aunt Helen is planning her one hundredth birthday for the 2005 Bash, when Peggy and I also hope to celebrate our 60th anniversary at Indiana's Turkey Run State Park.

Helen's oldest son, Austin Jones, PhD, retired after heading the psychology department at Arizona State University. However, his wife, Marion Kirk Jones, who is also retired from ASU, still dances and teaches dance as an octogenarian.

Their oldest, Cleve, has become widely known for his work with AIDS, including originating the monumental quilt.

His sister, Elizabeth, married John Ettinger, and they have daughters Frances and Sylvia.

Helen's second, Suzanne, married John Mulligan, retired United Airlines pilot. In addition to being Bash regulars and their multiple Bash hosting at Omena, Michigan, we have enjoyed many winter visits and duffer golf with them in Florida.

Traverse Bay

Their firstborn, Scott, married Karen Crippes. Both work for Apple Computers in San Jose, and they have children Kyle and Jack.

Second son, Dan, is married to Colleen Tennant, whose bagpipes have enlivened Bash attendees. Their children are Timothy and Cavan.

The youngest, Robert, married Natalia Gomez. Both are college teachers when Rob is not involved in a musical gig.

Last, but not least, of the Blythe/Helen Jones family was Sylvia, who married her old boss, Jim Hatton, now retired from his executive position with Ford Aerospace. They raised daughter Casey and son George in Costa Mesa, California, with the active involvement of Aunt Helen during recent years.

And this is my wonderful family!

At the beginning, I claimed to be writing, among other things, a love story–my love for Peggy, friends and family. I hope that element has spoken for itself, but knowing my limitations, let me close with Browning, who perhaps said it best:

How Do I Love Thee?
by Elizabeth Barrett Browning

How do I love thee? Let me count the ways.
I love thee to the depth and breadth and height
My soul can reach, when feeling out of sight
For the ends of Being and ideal Grace.

I love thee to the level of everyday's
Most quiet need, by sun and candlelight.
I love thee freely, as men strive for Right;
I love thee purely, as they turn from Praise

I love thee with the passion put to use
In my old griefs, and with my childhood's faith.
I love thee with a love I seemed to lose
With my lost saints – I love thee with the breath,
Smiles, tears, of all my life! – and, if God choose,
I shall but love thee better after death.

Postscript: As with the rediscovery of the Carlsons, the instant production of this book begins, there will be another wedding planned, news of a birth, or I will wish I had thanked another friend, told one more tale........Who knows? A second edition? Your denial or better version of the same slice of history? But for now, this is my story and I am sticking with it, grateful for the love and support of those who have lived it with me. It has been exciting to experience and fun to tell. Thanks to all!

Colophon

This book was printed on sixty pound Natures
Natural paper, Smyth sewn, and case bound by
Thomson-Shore, Inc. of Dexter, Michigan.
Typesetting in twelve point Times New Roman
and laser-printed camera-ready copy were by
Prairie Publications of Urbana, Illinois. Photo-
graphs were by Byron Evans with a Kodak 210
camera. Images were prepared with a Hewlett-
Packard 1210 scanner.